Romance Around the Corner

Romance Around the Corner

8 Steps Toward Attracting the Man of Your Dreams and Having Fun in the Process!

Valerie Beck

iUniverse, Inc.
New York Lincoln Shanghai

Romance Around the Corner
**8 Steps Toward Attracting the Man of Your Dreams
and Having Fun in the Process!**

Copyright © 2005 by Valerie Beck

All rights reserved. No part of this book may be used or reproduced by any means, graphic, electronic, or mechanical, including photocopying, recording, taping or by any information storage retrieval system without the written permission of the publisher except in the case of brief quotations embodied in critical articles and reviews.

iUniverse books may be ordered through booksellers or by contacting:

iUniverse
2021 Pine Lake Road, Suite 100
Lincoln, NE 68512
www.iuniverse.com
1-800-Authors (1-800-288-4677)

ISBN-13: 978-0-595-37083-2 (pbk)
ISBN-13: 978-0-595-67456-5 (cloth)
ISBN-13: 978-0-595-81483-1 (ebk)
ISBN-10: 0-595-37083-7 (pbk)
ISBN-10: 0-595-67456-9 (cloth)
ISBN-10: 0-595-81483-2 (ebk)

Printed in the United States of America

To the man of my dreams

Contents

Introduction	How I Went from Being the Dateless Wonder to Being the Girl Whose Phone Never Stops Ringing	ix
Get Ready!	The 8 Steps and the Philosophies Behind Them	xvii
Step 1	Love Yourself	1
Step 2	Know Who You Want, and Program Your Subconscious Mind to Attract Him	16
Step 3	Turn Up Your Feminine Energy	23
Step 4	Look and Feel Your Best	31
Step 5	Leave Your House	44
Step 6	Flirt, Flirt, Flirt!	53
Step 7	You've Got a Date! Now What?	59
Step 8	Be True To Yourself	74
Conclusion	Romance is Around the Corner	81

Introduction

How I Went from Being the Dateless Wonder to Being the Girl Whose Phone Never Stops Ringing

Let me share this fact with you from the beginning: I was not a natural at dating. My boyfriend/man of my dreams refuses to believe this, and for that I love him. But truly, I never used to believe that romance was around the corner, down the block, across town, or even necessarily on the other side of the world! I remember hearing years ago that everyone has 50,000 soulmates, and thinking that mine were probably dead, not born, or possibly living in Malaysia. I was not a natural at dating, but it's not where you start, it's where you finish.

Growing up, I was a dating failure, not because I failed on dates (that came later), but because I had none! In grammar school, I wasn't the popular girl surrounded by friends on the playground. I was shy and studious and had been reading books since age two. In junior high school, I wasn't the fun-loving natural flirt with the cool clothes whom everybody followed, admired, and envied. I had skipped two grades and was so tiny that my mother dressed me until 8th grade in Sesame Street clothes and Garanimals, which, you may recall, were adorable little mix-and-match outfits that our parents coordinated based on the animals on the tops and pants. The popular girls strutted off in packs to birthday parties and the mall in their Gloria Vanderbilt jeans; I walked alone to the library in my tops and pants with matching turtles on the pockets.

In high school, things went from bad to worse. I was a straight-A student at a school where boys could be simultaneously straight-A students and datable, while girls could be only one or the other. Cheerleaders were datable; geeks were not. I was a half-black, half-Jewish girl at a school in a wealthy white Chicago suburb where blacks and Jews couldn't join the local country club, even though the richest black man in Chicago owned an estate that backed up to the country club. I should mention too that while the suburb I went to school in was wealthy, my family was not. My father made a lot of money, but he kept it all when my parents divorced. It seemed that for years, my mother and my younger sister and brother and I ate nothing but soup and tuna salad that we made from tuna fish, mayonnaise, and pickle relish. My high school wasn't an all-kinds-of-everybody place like the ones in the movie *Fame* or the TV show *21 Jump Street*; it was more like the highly stratified high schools in Molly Ringwald movies like *Sixteen Candles* and *The Breakfast Club*.

In a nutshell, I was different in a time and place where different equaled undesirable. I remember a handsome boy in physics class who liked me and flirted with me until another boy told him I was "mixed." Can you believe that the fact of my fabulous heritage dumped cold water on the flames of his desire? Previously, I'd been thrilled when boys wanted to sit next to me in geometry class, but I soon realized it wasn't because they liked me; it was simply because they wanted to copy my notes once they found out that I got the highest score on every test. I felt as though cold water had been dumped on me.

So there I was, a tiny, unpopular, mixed-race geek-ette with no natural dating skills and as of yet no mindset to learn them. I'm here to give you hope! It's been said that we fail forward to success. Here's an overview of my against-the-odds dating success, from high school to the present:

I had absolutely no dates in high school. No prom, no homecoming, no Saturday night, no come over and study, nothing! I was cute, but undatable. During my four years of college, I had a grand total of five dates. Admittedly, Harvard wasn't exactly a party school, but still. And two of those five dates took place on my study-abroad program in Paris and possibly shouldn't even count, because the French boys wanted to date any American girl who spoke French. Things picked up in law school (even though Harvard Law School couldn't be described as a party school either), and I had five whole dates in one year. Now, that may or may not sound exciting to you, but it sure represented progress to me.

Why was I more datable? Because my mindset had begun to change. The Romance Around the Corner steps can help you change your mindset too.

After my first year of law school, at age 22, I got married. My first husband (I'm currently between husbands) was a handsome and kind young German lawyer I met during my summer clerkship in London, and we lived in Hamburg during most of our marriage. We had a pretty wonderful relationship until he slipped into schizophrenia and refused help. I tried to save him, but have you ever tried to save someone who didn't want saving? At age 29 I got divorced and came back to my hometown of Chicago. I was heartbroken, in the midst of a nervous breakdown, and clinically depressed. I thought melodramatically that I'd never love again. (Been there? Are there?) At that point, I wouldn't have gone on a date even if anyone had asked me, which most assuredly no one did.

After hibernating for a year I woke up—and started to grow up. I realized that the next decade could be better than the one that had just passed, and that indeed it had to be better. I needed a whole new life. I began using almost every dating aid in existence: Internet dating, speed dating, expensive matchmaking services, matchmaking services that are expensive for the man and free for the woman, blind dates, books about dating, voodoo (teasing, but I really would have tried just about anything). One of the biggest problems I found was that I was spending time and money by using these services, but I still wasn't meeting people with whom I was compatible, and I still didn't know what to do when I did meet someone. In other words, I went from dateless to clueless.

So, I decided to take matters into my own hands. I began reading books not about dating and relationships but about growth and personal development. I read Norman Vincent Peale's <u>The Power of Positive Thinking</u>. I read Napoleon Hill's <u>Think and Grow Rich</u>. I read Mary Kay Ash's autobiography <u>Miracles Happen</u>. I read books by Wayne Dyer, Anthony Robbins, Zig Ziglar, Ayanla Vanzant, and John Maxwell.

At the same time, I began making other positive changes in my life. I quit a draining and demoralizing 80-hour-a-week job as a corporate lawyer. You know it's time for a new job when, in addition to getting that sinking feeling Sundays at 4 pm, you're actually at the office Sundays at 4 pm. I took interior design classes. I started a business I was excited about with Mary Kay and grew it to the point where I now hold a leadership role. I picked up tennis again, then moved to taking ballet lessons again, and am now a Pilates junkie. I ran from negative people like I was running from a burning building and made new, positive friends.

As I changed myself, inside and out, I began attracting men. Nice men! Handsome men! Stable men! Fun men! Romantic men! Gentlemen! I could barely believe it myself, but I was being asked out on dates! I tinkered with and fine-tuned my attraction process, entirely through trial and error and error and error, and I didn't give up. I decided that I was going to have a rich and wonderful dating life, and I decided I was going to meet the man of my dreams. Other people seemed to; why not me?

Today, after refining my attraction and dating activity into 8 steps and having woven the 8 steps into my life, I get stopped on the street by men who want my number. Men follow me into cafes to meet me. Men send drinks over when I'm at a restaurant. Men write me notes. The other day a man followed me out of the bank to tell me he liked my freckles. Ex-boyfriends call me, hoping for another chance. (One just called as I was writing this!)

What changed? Men? Of course not! You know and I know that men do not change. Men become more deeply who they already are, and when we find a man we love, we must love him for who he is. I repeat: men didn't change; I did. I found that when you change your attitude, you change your life.

I am now dating the man of my dreams. He came walking toward me one day. My heart stopped, my breathing stopped, and every cell in my body felt magnetized toward him. When my brain started working again, I thought, "It's Cary Grant!" And he says that when he saw me, he thought, "Who the hell is that? She's gorgeous!" Who is this amazing man of my dreams? Imagine Cary Grant crossed with Mick Jagger. He's a dashing gentleman with a rock-star edge. He's a bad boy with a heart of gold. He's romantic and he's masculine. He's wildly successful and he's successfully wild. He's brilliant and he's playful. He's rough and he's tender. He's sexy and he's wise. He's hot and he's cool! Best of all, no one has ever treated me so well.

Are you thinking, "Wow, that's great for her, but that could never happen for me?" This book isn't about patting myself on the back. This book is about the fact that if the 8 steps work for a geeky, burnt-out, ex-clinically depressed, recovering attorney, they can work for you too. And wouldn't you agree that you have nothing to lose and everything to gain? The man of your dreams is alive and walking the Earth. Meeting him is partially about being in the right place at the right time, but it is also about being in the right frame of mind. If you're in the right place at the right time but with the wrong attitude, good luck. If you've got the right frame of mind, you can draw him to where you are. Stop thinking a good man is hard to find, and let him find you.

This book will help you be your best you, so that you can attract the best man for you. This book will give you specific tips on attracting the kind of man you want to attract, and on what to do once you attract him. You might need to start scouting around for a great cell phone plan, because you'll need the minutes when your phone starts ringing with calls from one eligible bachelor after another. Whether you're a dateless wonder like I used to be, or whether you're a dating diva, there is more out there for you. Romance is around the corner, and it's your turn!

Get Ready!

The 8 Steps and the Philosophies Behind Them

The 8 steps to getting dates galore, having successful dates, and attracting the man of your dreams not only work, they're fun! The 8 steps to Romance Around the Corner are below, and we'll look at each one more closely in subsequent chapters:

- Step 1: Love Yourself

- Step 2: Know Who You Want, and Program Your Subconscious Mind to Attract Him

- Step 3: Turn Up Your Feminine Energy

- Step 4: Look and Feel Your Best

- Step 5: Leave Your House

- Step 6: Flirt, Flirt, Flirt!

- Step 7: You've Got a Date! Now What?

- Step 8: Be True to Yourself

Before we jump into the 8 steps, which I drew from old wisdom, common sense, and things our mothers told us, let me tell you the philosophies behind them.

Philosophy #1: Don't believe the negative hype.

First, I decided I wasn't going to believe the anti-happiness statistics. What anti-happiness statistics? You know them. They're the ones that say we're less likely to meet a man than we are to be struck by lightning twice while rollerblading backward in the desert. Or that after 30, your chances of getting married plummet like Chicago temperatures in December. Nonsense! I don't use profanity, but I will quote Mark Twain, who said that there are lies, damned lies, and statistics. Abraham Lincoln said that most people are about as happy as they make up their minds to be. I decided I would believe the old adage that there's someone for everyone. I took as my motto and mantra the statement that the man of my dreams is alive and walking the Earth, and that I am attracting him to me just as surely as if I were a planet exercising my gravitational pull. And, when people said that because I was divorced I'd have a harder time maneuvering through the dating world and finding a second husband, I ignored those people and figured that I was in good company: 50% of everyone else who got married is apparently divorced too. Whatever your views on the current state of marriage in America, the fact of the matter is that there is new inventory coming onto the market all the time.

Philosophy #2: Seek and ye shall find.

Next, I decided not to listen to the people who told me I'd find a man when I wasn't looking. Have you ever found an apartment when you weren't looking? Or a job? Or your keys? If you wanted a new job, would you just stay put on the sofa and tell yourself you'd find that new job when you weren't looking? Or would you call your contacts, call a recruiter, update your resume, scour the newspapers and the online job sites, tell your friends to keep their eyes open, and generally get up and get into action? I decided I would believe the wise old advice "seek and ye shall find."

Philosophy #3: You must give to get.

It is a law of the universe that you must give before you can receive. You must plant seeds before you can reap the harvest. When men weren't asking me out, I started putting a few questions to myself: How many men have I smiled at today? How many events or activities have I participated in this week? How often have I been anywhere besides home or the office this month? Stay at home and stay negative, and that will be your reality. Expand your thinking and your actions, and you expand your possibilities and your life. Like a boomerang, whatever you send out comes back to you.

Philosophy #4: You get what you expect.

You've heard of self-fulfilling prophecies. We tend to think of them in terms of negative things coming true. For example, when you expect to gain weight, there are the pounds. When you expect to stumble as you're coming down the stairs, oops, there you go. But self-fulfilling prophecies don't have to be negative; you can create positive self-fulfilling prophecies. Someone wise said that the best way to predict the future is to create it. What if you tell yourself that blessings are chasing you down and overtaking you? That your higher power wants only the best for you? That you are here on this planet for a bigger purpose than being miserable and suffering and dying? That the universe is plotting in your favor to make your dreams come true? What if you expect miracles? What if you expect abundance? What if you expect the man of your dreams? I decided I could make romantic love a self-fulfilling prophecy.

Philosophy #5: You attract who you are.

Another great adage is that water seeks its own level. Have you ever noticed that most couples resemble or match each other? If he's elegantly dressed, so is she. If she's casual or sporty, so is he. I once met a couple who were each tattooed over about half of their bodies. Like attracts like. Be geeky and attract geeks. Be neurotic and attract someone whose neuroses play off of yours. Be desperate and attract a desperate loser. Think you're a nobody, and attract nobody. Be happy, confident, and fabulous, and attract someone truly wonderful! This is the attitude that pervades the book and weaves throughout the 8 steps. You can do it, and I'm about to show you how.

One final note before we turn to the first of the 8 Romance Around the Corner steps: if anything you read in this book sounds strange or corny and you don't feel like trying it, don't try it for 3 months, and then try it for 3 months, and then ask yourself why you didn't try it 6 months ago! You've probably heard the saying that the definition of insanity is doing the same thing and expecting different results. If you're not currently getting the results you want in your dating life, try something else, because nothing will change until you change something. We're going to shake up your routine and start you on positive habits. If something seems corny at first, it won't after it works. The 8 steps work for me; let them work for you! Email me at romancearoundthecorner@yahoo.com and let me know how it's going.

Step 1

Love Yourself

Success is an inside job. Nothing is more attractive than a happy, confident personality shining out of a genuine smile. Dating and being in relationships are wonderful when those relationships enhance your already fantastic life. You are a masterpiece all by yourself, and a superb man can enhance your superb life as you enhance his. But the person you most want to love is you. If you don't love you, why should anyone else? You will attract your dream man from a position of love and satisfaction with your own life, not from a position of lack and desperation. Like attracts like. Be confident, and you'll attract someone confident. Be needy and unhealthy, and you'll attract someone whose insecurities feed off of yours. Be proud and fun and fabulous, and you'll meet your match! A man followed me into a café one day, sat down next to me, and said he just had to meet me. I said, "Hi, my name is Valerie." We got to know each other and ended up dating for a couple of months. When I asked him what made him want to meet me, he said that as I was walking down Michigan Avenue, I looked happy and kind and had positive energy all around me. Exude love, and love will find you!

Raise Your Self-Esteem

Are you exuding love right now? Are you someone who lights up a room, or do you slip in unnoticed and slip out the same way? Are people happy to see you, or happy to see you leave? Do you let your light shine, or is your confidence level not exactly a beacon for others? The good news is that you can fake it 'til you make it! If you wouldn't date yourself, you can't blame others for not feeling amorous toward you either. Or maybe you're currently a model of self-esteem for all of us, in which case you too can take it up a notch. How many people in the history of the planet have reached their full potential? There's always room for growth. If you and your life aren't feeling fantastic, you can do something about it, and if you do feel great, you can feel greater.

When I emerged into the dating world after my divorce—I can't say that I "re-emerged" because I hadn't really known what I was doing before—my self-confidence wasn't at its peak. I made a conscious decision to boost my self-image because I knew that if I didn't feel great about myself, I'd settle for someone who didn't feel great about himself either, and we'd have a relationship that wasn't great. But if instead I worked toward becoming a better person and having a better attitude, the world—and the pick of the men in it—would be mine. Here is what I did and what I invite you to do to raise your level of happiness, confidence, and self-esteem:

1. <u>Make a list of your good points</u>. If you can't think of any, keep reading. Just start where you are. Your list could be as simple as

"nice teeth," or "good friend," or "can carry a tune." Or, perhaps your list contains items such as "beautiful inside and out," "enthusiastic personality," or "never gives up on a dream." Add to this list as often as possible, and put this list in a rainy day file that you can pull out anytime you need a lift. Every human contains seeds of greatness. Look within and begin to discover more greatness than you ever thought possible.

2. <u>Ask friends and family what they love about you</u>. Be sure, though, that you ask people whom you know will give you glowing reviews. If there's doubt, don't ask. And get ready to be surprised and even overwhelmed by the wonderful responses you get. The people who love you might love things about you that you don't see in yourself or don't value. Get your reviews in writing; then you can add them to your rainy day file and look at them whenever you want. When others believe in you, you can lean on that belief and let it strengthen your own.

3. <u>Trash your house with affirmations</u>. An affirmation is a positive, personal, present tense description of how you want the world to be. Put sticky notes up all over that say "I'm happy, I'm attractive, and I'm in demand!" Put these notes on your mirror, refrigerator, dashboard, datebook, and other places where you will be confronted with them. Surround yourself with them, and you'll believe them! Your subconscious mind doesn't know the difference between fact and fiction, and it will believe whatever you tell it as it goes to work to complete whatever picture you paint it. So,

paint positive pictures and keep this positivity in front of you as often as possible.

4. <u>Keep a gratitude notebook</u>. Every day, write down three things you're grateful for. When I began this exercise some years ago, I was so depressed that my list read "I have a bed, I'm breathing, and I have my arms and legs." Start where you are, and be grateful for what you do have, whether it's little or much. As the saying goes, be grateful for what you have, and you'll soon have more to be grateful for.

5. <u>Put a spring in your step and a sparkle in your eye</u>. Walk like you're happy and excited to get somewhere, and your internal feelings will begin to mirror your external presentation. When you smile and move with a confident gait, your brain produces chemicals to make you feel happy. When you frown, your brain goes to work to make your inside as depressed as your outside. So look alive! Notice your environment; curiosity about the world around you puts a sparkle in your eye. Instead of focusing entirely on your interior worries or state of mind, put your attention on others. Look at beautiful things. Notice the people walking by. Notice the faces of the people at your lunchtime café. Be grateful you can perceive your surroundings, and be excited about them.

6. <u>Act enthusiastic to become enthusiastic</u>. Look for the good in every situation, and look for the good in yourself. We've all heard the saying that every cloud has a silver lining. Look for *your* silver lining. Charity starts at home, and change starts from within.

Be excited about who you are and who you are becoming. Even if you don't feel it at first, be an actress and act thrilled about yourself and your life. This attitude will take root and grow if you nurture and practice it, and pretty soon your self-esteem will rise to meet your expectation. Optimists live longer and better than pessimists. We date more often too! If you think being optimistic means being a Pollyanna, you're wrong. Read Norman Vincent Peale's book <u>The Tough-Minded Optimist</u>, in which he explains that the optimist is someone who knows that there is bad in the world, but who believes in the preponderance of good and actively seeks it out. It takes moral courage to be happy in a sad world, and to be positive in a negative world. Choose courage. Let positive people, books, movies, and CDs help you. Let enthusiasm in, and enthusiasm will shine out!

7. <u>Flirt with yourself</u>. Every time you pass a mirror, say "hello, gorgeous!" Extra points if you say it out loud! I watch very little TV because it typically does nothing to enhance the important areas of my life—faith, love, family, and career—but I once saw an episode of a reality TV show about young actors and actresses trying to make it in Hollywood. One of the acting hopefuls had a ritual in which she looked into the mirror and said words to the effect of, "I am too beautiful, I am too sexy, I am too smart, I am too dedicated, and I am too wonderful. With all of those 'toos,' I must be a perfect ten!" With her positive attitude and persistence, I felt sure she was going to make it.

8. <u>Give to others</u>. A wonderful way to feel good about yourself is to do something good for someone else. This takes you out of yourself and connects you with the wider world, and as you spread joy, joy returns to you. Whatever you send into the world comes back to you in abundance. Giving could be as simple as giving some coins to someone on the street who asks you if you can spare some change. Or, do something nice for your mother or sister. Call a long-distance friend and tell her you were thinking of her. Give your barista a tip. Sign up at your church or a local school to tutor a child. Pay a stranger a compliment. Call your favorite family member and say "I love you." Treat others the way you would like to be treated, and watch new doors open in your life.

Give and Take

If you want a garden, it won't help to sit and stare at the earth and hope that a garden grows. Hope is not a strategy. You've got to plant some seeds and water them in order to get a garden. You must give before you receive, and you will reap what you sow. You've probably heard the phrases "to have a friend, be a friend," and "God helps those who help themselves." You never get something for nothing, and if it's worth having it's worth paying the price. To have love, give love. Love yourself, and that love will radiate out from you and return back to you in abundance.

Along those lines, if men aren't asking you out, ask yourself, "How many men have I smiled at today?" How many events or activities have you participated in this week? How often this month have you been somewhere other than your apartment or your office? Do your part, and the universe will do its part. We will look more closely in Step 5 at where to go and what to do once you get there, but for now, simply start giving, and be open to receiving. To inhale, we must exhale, and to exhale, we must inhale. When we inhale, we don't try to hold the air in for fear that this could be our last breath. And when we exhale, we never worry in letting go of that breath that there might not another one available. We give and take in the abundance of the world through breathing, through helping others, through participating in the economy, and through countless other ways including through our relationships. There is more than enough oxygen to spare, and more than enough men.

Don't worry that your dream man doesn't exist, or that all of the good ones are taken or gay, or that you'll never find anyone for you, or that your biological clock will tick out. That is negative, scarcity thinking, and it produces nothing but negativity and scarcity. Plant turnips and you will harvest turnips. Plant roses, and you will have a beautiful rose garden. We live in an abundant world, our higher power wants us to be happy and fulfilled as we reach to develop our potential, and it's raining men! Have a glass-half-full mentality. There is someone for everyone. And whatever you think about the 50% divorce rate in America in recent years, the truth is that new men and new possibilities become available every day.

Raise Your Deserve Level

You've heard of people who won the lottery and then lost all of their money within a few years. What happened? It could be poor financial advice, poor spending habits, or the simple fact that we never receive or hold onto more than we think we deserve. No one on earth is greater than you, and you deserve the best! To have it, you must believe it. With a high deserve level, you not only attract and keep the best, you also are able to let go of what doesn't meet your standards. In other words, if you know you deserve to be treated like a queen, you won't put up with anyone who treats you like dirt, and you will hold out for your king. I once dated a man who kept disappearing from my life and then reappearing when it was convenient for him. Truth be told, I can't really call that "dating." In any case, I finally said enough is enough, told him I was going to be with someone who was going to be with me, and no longer called him back. There were enough men to call back who wanted to treat me like a queen.

I raised my deserve level by doing the following things, and I encourage you to do them too:

1. <u>Pay attention to your mental health by monitoring your self-talk</u>. Did a voice in your head just say, "What does she mean by self-talk?" That voice is your self-talk, which is your consciousness. It is the constant commentary on what we see, hear, do, and think. Sometimes our self-talk is based on old recordings that run in our head that tell us we're not good enough, or that our sister is the

popular one, or that the goal is impossible. These old recordings might have come from well-meaning parents or teachers, or from ill-meaning kids on the playground, or from any number of people close to us, and these tapes can be so insidious and pernicious that we might not even realize that they're there or how much damage they're doing. The good news is that you control the remote. You can rewind, eject, or record a new message over the old ones. But first you've got to realize that those messages are there. So start listening in on yourself, as it were, and be aware of your self-talk. To fix a problem, it helps to know what it is.

2. <u>Eliminate negative words from your vocabulary and replace them with positive words</u>. As you become more aware of your self-talk, begin adjusting it. Some child-rearing experts believe that for every negative thing you tell a child, you must tell him or her four positive things. The human mind seems to sink easily into negativity, whereas positivity requires active choice, vigilance, and discipline. Does the price for positivity seem high? The price for negativity is higher. If you want a happy life with the man of your dreams, you can't afford the luxury of doubt and negativity. Replace "I can't" with "I can, I will, I must!" Replace "impossible" with "let's get started!" Replace negative talk with positive talk immediately and constantly.

3. <u>Run from negative people like you're running from a burning building</u>. I've read that when people die in fires, it's more often from smoke inhalation than from being burnt. Negativity is like

smoke: it will choke you and take you under before you even know what hit you. Does it seem like we're spending a lot of time on creating a positive mental attitude? Good! We are indeed spending a lot of time on attitude because your attitude, more than anything else, will determine your ability to attract wonderful men. Have you heard the saying that attitude is 90% of success and technique is 10%? Wouldn't you agree that this applies to just about everything in life? Your friends are like buttons on an elevator in that they'll take you up, or they'll take you down. Make a list of the five people you spend the most time with. After spending time with them, do you feel better or worse about yourself and the world? When I first did this exercise several years ago, I read my list and got so depressed I wanted to go lie down. Today I have friends who are motivated, positive, energetic people, and we enrich each others' lives and cheer each other on in the dating arena and beyond.

4. <u>Dream about what you want your life to be</u>. Think big! When you were a little girl, what did you dream about? Being a princess? Being president? I know a fourteen-year-old girl whose plans include Stanford Law School, women's basketball championships, a political career, a save-the-animals foundation, and ownership of a horse ranch in South Carolina. Does it seem that sometimes life squeezes the imagination out of us, and that those little-girl dreams get shoved into the back of the closet? Pull them out, dust them off, and make them bigger and better than ever.

Dream about your dream man and your dream life. Read inspirational biographies about people like Wilma Rudolph, who overcame polio, poverty, and Jim Crow segregation to become a track champion and the first American woman to win three gold medals at the Olympics. Instead of focusing on the problem, focus on the solution. Instead of settling for the crumbs that circumstances give you, change your circumstances by changing your mind. Step up to the banquet table. We live in an abundant world, and there is more than enough love, money, and everything else to share and to spare. You can draw abundance to you by first thinking about the abundance you want to enjoy. As someone wise once said, nothing happens but first a dream.

5. <u>Make a plan, and start</u>. Sometimes action precedes belief instead of the other way around. This book gives you the plan; all you have to do is hit the gas. Are you simply reading the exercises in this book, or are you actually doing them? When you take up a new sport or hobby, or learn a new language, isn't it usually hard at first? But as you keep going, your belief in your ability grows as your ability grows. When you see small victories, you start to believe that larger ones are possible. So begin, be consistent, and don't give up. As my mother taught me, when the going gets tough, the tough get going!

6. <u>Improve your mental health by saying affirmations</u>. An affirmation is a positive, personal, present-tense statement about how you want the world to be. For example, if you want to lose weight, a

good affirmation is not "I'm going to lose 20 pounds of ugly fat," but rather, "I love looking and feeling my ideal weight of ___ pounds." Instead of "Someday I'm going to have a date," make your affirmation powerful by saying "I love dating wonderful gentlemen" or "I love being happily married to the man of my dreams." Why are affirmations so important? Because your mind believes whatever you tell it. Just as you are what you eat, you are what you think about all day. Feed your mind negative, poisonous thoughts, and reap a bitter harvest. Feed your mind wishy-washy, inconsistent thoughts, and get a wishy-washy life. Feed your mind strong, specific, healthy, positive pictures, and your mind will go to work to turn those pictures into reality. It's been said that we don't always get what we want, but we usually get what we expect. Expect to have a wonderful dating life, and let your affirmations pave the way!

7. <u>Do something you love every day</u>. Why? Because this tells your mind and the universe that you're worth it. Plus, it makes you happy, and you deserve to be happy. If you spend all day every day taking care of others at home and on the job, and you spend no time on yourself, you are reinforcing the message that you're not worthy of care or loving treatment. A stressed-out woman is not an asset to her man (or potential man), her family, her job, or herself. Are you under stress or above your stress? Doing something you love helps put problems in perspective and makes you more important than your problems. And, how can you pour from

an empty cup? Fill your cup. Let your cup runneth over. Take time for yourself daily—even if it's simply relaxing in a bubble bath for 15 minutes or buying a yellow tulip for your desk—and you'll reinforce the idea that you deserve good things to flow to you. Change your mind, and you'll change your habits; change your habits, and you'll change your life. When you take the time to be good to yourself, you're taking the time to trust in yourself and in your source, be it God, the universe, or whatever your own higher power is.

8. <u>Pay attention to your physicality</u>. Improve your posture, watch your nutrition, get enough sleep, and exercise. Good posture and good physical habits tell the world and yourself that you respect and love yourself. And if you do, others will too. Beautiful skin and a beautiful figure certainly won't hurt in attracting a man, but even more important is simply that you are comfortable in your own self. When my marriage and life were falling apart under my first husband's mental illness and my confusion about what to do, I became so nervous and frightened that I couldn't sleep and lost my appetite. I dropped down to 92 pounds, I felt sick all the time, and I looked unwell. I remember looking in the mirror and thinking that I looked 50. There's nothing wrong with looking 50 if you're 60, but I was 29! My skin looked green, I had circles under my eyes, my face looked like a skeleton's, my doctor said I was in the danger zone, and when my mother hugged me all she could feel were bones. A trip to the hospital inspired me to change. I

joined a gym, worked out with a trainer, drank the protein-boosted smoothies she prescribed, and reclaimed my health step by step. I realized that my job as a corporate attorney at one of Chicago's biggest law firms was holding me back because not only was I utterly without passion for the work or the people with whom I worked, but I worked such long hours that if I slept 5 hours a night I was lucky. Have you ever noticed that a tired mind rarely makes good decisions and hardly ever has a positive attitude? I downshifted to a job with more reasonable hours, started telling people who asked what I did that I was a "future ex-lawyer," and eventually left that firm too. Today I have a career that I love, I set my own hours, I get enough sleep, I stand up straight and proud at almost 5 feet 2 inches (5' 4" in heels), I eat right and believe that eating right includes eating chocolate, and I exercise every day. I know that every day my body can become better or worse, and that it's my choice. Similarly, my attitude can become better or worse every day, and it's my choice. My mind and body are connected, and each of them is the only one I've got, so I take care of them and love them. Let your joy in being you manifest itself through excellent physical habits. In Mary Kay we say, "Take time now, or time will take you later."

To sum up, Step 1 of the Romance Around the Corner plan is to develop your love for yourself. This is an ongoing step, and you develop self-love by raising your self-esteem and your deserve level. Be grateful, be enthusiastic, and believe in yourself. Always be green and growing. Just as we never master breathing in the sense that we can't stop breathing one day and yet keep living and growing, loving yourself is an ongoing process, and it's a process that deepens in joy and effectiveness as you continue to practice it. Feel great about yourself and you've got an underpinning that allows you not only to attract the man of your dreams, but also—to paraphrase Rudyard Kipling—to meet triumph and disaster with appropriate equanimity, to attract abundance into your life, and quite simply to become the person you were meant to be.

Step 2

Know Who You Want, and Program Your Subconscious Mind to Attract Him

You've heard of self-fulfilling prophecies, right? For example, have you ever felt certain you'd spill your drink at a fancy dinner, and then you did? Or do you know someone who says that everything she eats turns to fat, and it does? Well, although it might not be as well-publicized, self-fulfilling prophecies work for good things as well as bad. In every aspect of life, we may not always get what we want, but we usually get what we expect. So, expect the best! You deserve it! What if you made enjoying an exciting dating life and meeting your dream man a self-fulfilling prophecy? What if you made the fulfillment of your dreams and goals an inevitability? What if you told yourself that the man of your dreams is alive and walking the Earth, and that the two of you are bound to bump into each other? Your subconscious mind can help you.

But first, you've got to know exactly what you want. How will the universe know whom to send you if it doesn't know who you want?

Actress and comedienne Lily Tomlin once said, "I always wanted to be somebody. I guess I should have been more specific." You might be hoping for George Clooney or Denzel Washington, but if you don't tell the universe, why shouldn't it send you Elmer Fudd?

Make Your "Man List"

How to be clear about exactly who you want? Make a list. List-making works to clarify your mind and focus your actions, whether you're making a grocery list, a list of research ideas for your Ph.D., a list of financial goals, a list of your top 10 things to do during your lifetime, or your Man List. Simply begin writing down all of the characteristics you want your dream man to have. Make your Man List as detailed and specific as you like. You can include personality type, physical characteristics, religious or spiritual tendencies, character traits, Myers-Briggs type, humor or seriousness, how much he loves you, lifestyle, goals, marital status, and anything else you choose. Nothing is too outrageous, or too petty, or too unrealistic. Dream, and put your dreams on paper.

A friend of mine made her Man List and met the man who is now her husband. She showed him the list, and he said, "Babe, that's me." Another friend of mine complained that she never met anyone. I asked who her dream man was, and she said she didn't know. I asked her how she would know when she met him if she didn't know who he was. A lightbulb seemed suddenly to go off over her head, and she started thinking about what she would put on her Man List.

After I first made my Man List, I started attracting the kind of man I wanted: Cary Grant. Where did all of these tall, dark, handsome, sophisticated, elegant, well-dressed, hilarious, and down-to-earth men come from? They were there all along, but I wasn't ready for them until I went through the trial and error and adventures and misadventures that resulted in the 8 steps. When I learned who I wanted and how to attract him, he began to appear in various forms. And interestingly, I stopped meeting men who were completely wrong for me. No longer did I seem to be watching a seemingly random parade of variegated individuals who had nothing in common except for the fact that I had nothing in common with them. Instead, I encountered man after man who had a good shot. Man after man who was in the realm of the possible. Man after man who was some version of the man on my Man List. I said to myself, "I'm getting closer!"

Do you believe that miracles and opportunities are all around us, and that we must open our eyes and be ready to see and receive them? Do you believe that we do not see what we do not believe in? I believe that possibilities surround us, and that the people we need and want are around us. We must simply recognize them.

Does all of this sound too simple? Make your own Man List and see. In fact, this is crucial. Skip one of the 8 steps, and you'll likely have spotty, inconsistent results. Make that Man List! Write it in the margin of this book. Write it on a receipt that you fish out of your purse. Get a pen, get some paper, and make that list. For the power of intention and attraction to work, you have to know whom you intend to attract. Let me give you an analogy. If you want to listen to National Public Radio in Chicago, you tune in to 91.5 FM. If you're wishy-washy about setting your radio, and you end up on 91.3 or 91.8, you'll get a wishy-washy signal. Have only a vague idea of the kind of man you'll be happy with, and you might get a motley collection of vague characters crossing your path, as used to be my experience. (Been there? Are there?) Set your dial to the exact frequency of the kind of man you desire, and you'll receive signals that are loud and clear.

Program Your Subconscious Mind and Wake Up in Your Dream

It's important to put your Man List on paper because this helps you develop clarity as to exactly whom you want. Writing your list down shows that you are serious. Plus, the universe reads your writing better than it reads your mind. Make sure that you can read your writing too—type your list if need be—because you'll want to read your list every night before you fall asleep, and every morning before you get out of bed. Why? Because this lets you tap into the power of your subconscious mind, the most powerful force known to humanity. Your subconscious mind accepts as true whatever you give it, so give it exactly what you want to be true.

Now take it to the next level: after you read your list in bed at night, tell yourself, as you're drifting off to sleep, that the man described on your list is alive and walking the Earth, and that you are attracting him to you just as surely as if you were a planet exercising your gravitational pull.

Then, tell yourself that maybe you're dreaming right now, and that when you wake up in the morning you might wake up with your dream husband next to you in reality. What if your life without your dream man is the dream, and the reality is that you're already living a fabulous life with him? Take it to the hilt. Imagine that your dream husband is there with you, in your dream house, on your dream 900-count sheets, with your dream clothes in the closet, and your dream shoes in your special dream shoe closet. Imagine that you're about to wake up and go to your dream work, which enriches the lives of others as it enriches your own. Imagine your ideal life, with man, shoes, fulfillment, and all. Sounds insane? Sounds too metaphysical to work? It is actually practical advice. Your subconscious mind can be put to work for you or against you; it's your choice. If what you've been doing hasn't been giving you the results you'd like, what have you got to lose by trying something different, especially when this plan has worked for me and for others? And when you read your Man List every night, you'll probably have sweet dreams, wouldn't you agree?

When you wake up in the morning, wake up slowly. Before you open your eyes, paint the picture of your dream again, and tell yourself you'll wake up in your dream. Then open one eye, open the other eye, and smile. Start the day with positive energy, no matter what. George Bernard Shaw said, "First I make up my mind; then I make up my bed." If you wake up and your dream is actually reality, and your dream man is waking up beside you, rejoice! If he isn't there, rejoice anyway, because today could be the day you meet him. Tell yourself in the morning that maybe today will be the day, and spring out of bed with a smile. Be happy in the knowledge that a great day awaits you and that every second of every minute brings you closer to your dream man. He's dreaming about you too.

To sum up Step 2, let's recap as to how to know who you want and how to program your subconscious mind to attract him:

1. Make your Man List.

2. Read your list in bed every night and every morning. Bookend your dreams with your list, and you'll have sweet dreams, and sweet awakenings.

3. Tell yourself that the man on your list exists. In fact, he probably exists not just once but in a variety of forms! It's been said that everyone has 50,000 soulmates. All you need is one—or possibly one after another!

4. Tell yourself that you are attracting the man on your list as though you were a magnet, or as though you were a planet exercising gravitational pull.

5. Tell yourself that when you wake up in the morning, you might wake up to find that your dream is actually reality.

6. If you wake up and he's there, great! If he's not there, that's great too, because today could be the day you run into him. Tell yourself it's bound to happen one day, so why not today?

The subconscious is a fertile garden. You can plant turnips or roses, but you can't plant turnips and expect roses. Nor can you plant roses in faith and dig them up in fear. In other words, if you start and stop the plan, instead of working it consistently, you won't get the same results that you get if you stick with it. It takes 21 days to form a habit. Once you form a habit, it's hard to break. So commit to forming positive habits, such as reading your Man List morning and night, which will help you attract the man you desire.

Step 3

Turn Up Your Feminine Energy

I know you're familiar with the sensation of feeling someone's eyes upon you, and with the sensation of looking at someone and having that person turn and look back at you, as if by magic. We have more capacity to be in tune with our environment and with each other than we know. I bet you've also had the experience of feeling a positive or negative "vibe" from someone, or of sensing what is in that person's mind. What do these phenomena have to do with attracting men? Lots! Men can feel your feminine energy the same way that you can feel someone looking at you or feel a particular vibe from someone. What is your feminine energy? It is your joy in being a woman and your openness to the world around you—including your openness to finding a man. Men can sense whether you are comfortable in your skin and whether you are receptive to their advances. Turn up your feminine energy, and men will feel the pull.

Feminine Energy in Action

I heard somewhere that Marilyn Monroe was once walking down the street with a friend who marveled that no one recognized the gorgeous movie star he was with. Marilyn Monroe said, "Watch this." Suddenly, everyone started rushing up to her and exclaiming, "It's Marilyn Monroe!" What did she do to go from invisible to irresistible? My guess is that she turned up her feminine energy.

Here's an example from my own experience: Once I was at a chic restaurant in Chicago with my mother, aunt, and cousin. I had my feminine energy turned up because you never know whom you might meet when you're out and about. As I sat at our table, I felt eyes on me, but when I looked around, I couldn't see anyone who was paying the slightest bit of attention to me. All through dinner, I had the feeling that someone was looking at me, but I saw no one looking my way. The feeling of eyes on the back of my neck caused me to run my fingers across my neck, take off and put on my scarf, and adjust my hair. Still, no one appeared to be looking at me, so I chalked the feeling up to some sort of sensory hallucination and tried to stop fidgeting. Then when we asked for the check, the waiter said that one of the gentlemen who had just left the table behind us had already paid it. It took a moment for this to sink in, and then my mother grabbed my arm and shrieked, "Where'd he go?" I remembered that when I walked in, I had smiled demurely at the men at the table behind ours, and at the room in general, as I always do when entering a room. One of the men at that table must have been the one whose eyes I felt on the back of my neck throughout dinner. Whoever my mystery check-payer was, thank you!

Turn It Up!

Ready to turn up your feminine energy? Here are some ways to do it:

1. <u>Think pink and watch the mercury rise</u>. Visual images can make anything more powerful. Imagine a pink thermostat with a pink mercury display. Turn the dial, and watch the pink mercury of your feminine energy go up, up, up! Feel energized, happy, and attractive as it rises. While I was writing a draft of this section, I was sitting in a Starbucks in Chicago's Loop. My feminine energy rose as I wrote this, and a man came over and started talking to me. He was a cop who worked in a courtroom in the building, and he was very charming and sweet. After he left, he phoned the Starbucks to ask the barista to give me his phone number!

2. <u>Look pumped instead of slumped</u>. Didn't our mothers always tell us to stand up straight? Your feminine energy can best shine forth when your posture is open and when you are breathing deeply, rather than when your body language is closed and tense. When you model the posture of a happy, confident person, you begin to feel like one. Your brain creates chemicals to bring your interior and exterior states into harmony. Slouch, frown, and look at the ground, and you begin to feel tired and down. Look up, smile, and stand up straight, and you begin to feel positive and energized. Throughout the day, when standing, sitting, or walking, perform a

check of your posture. Are you slumped or pumped? Inhale deeply, and let your breath straighten you up. Exhale and grow yet taller, and let your feminine energy radiate through you and out into the world. Take up Pilates, yoga, or tai chi to help get your energy flowing and to help you focus on your physicality. More than aerobics or running, these activities develop a long, lean figure for you, they encourage you to focus on deep breathing and even learn different styles of breathing, and they help inspire a feminine energy that is gentle yet strong. If you're a Pilates junkie like me, you know that at the end of a session, you feel energized rather than depleted. Try a Pilates class and see!

3. <u>Grin and love it</u>. What expression is on your face when you think no one is looking? Do you look tense? Do you frown? Stop it! If you're worrying about money or your job or anything else, leave it at home; leave it at the office. When you're out and about, use that time to open your mind and spirit. Put a look on your face that invites smiles, positive energy, blessings, and friendly conversation, or that at the very least doesn't contribute to the negativity in the world. If you had to approach someone who was frowning or someone who was smiling, who would you choose? Try walking around with a gentle grin all day, as though you're on the verge of breaking into a megawatt smile, or as though someone might be filming you for your big television moment. Notice the favorable responses you get. One of the best ways to get people to like you

is by liking them. Send friendly energy out, and friendly energy will return to you.

4. <u>Be aware of eyes on you</u>. When someone looks at you, feel the eyes on you, and look back. You can just smile and keep going if you like, but if you're aware of your surroundings and who's in them, you send out energy that lets men know you're alive, awake, enthusiastic, and open for a smile or a hello. I was walking with a girlfriend one afternoon, and a man walking toward us started checking her out, as they say. He looked like he wanted to say hi to her, but she had a cranky, inward-focused look on her face. After he passed by, I asked if she noticed that the man who just walked by was looking her over. She looked up, surprised, and said, "What man?" An opportunity missed. Open up, and when you feel eyes on you, it's the perfect opportunity to practice the Shy Eye Flirt, which we'll cover in Chapter 6.

5. <u>Notice others</u>. Give out smiles and compliments to men, women, and children. It costs nothing, and you'll make someone's day while enhancing your positive energy. Expect nothing in return, and you'll be amazed at the positive results you receive in return, and at the way your whole day can go better. When your energy is focused not inward on your own problems and circumstances but outward to the world, you send out positive energy that attracts others to you. Who would *you* find more attractive: a stressed-out man who scurries around worrying about his own little world, or a

confident man who is comfortable in his environment and comfortable enough in his own skin to be concerned about others?

6. <u>Look alive</u>! Put a sparkle in your eye and a spring in your step. Be an alert part of your environment, and walk like you're happy and excited to get somewhere. Everyone loves to be around enthusiastic people, so be one. If you saw yourself walking down the street, would you say, "Wow, who's that happy, confident woman, and where is she going?" or would you even notice? Whatever you send out into the world will come back to you in abundance, so be proud to be a woman, turn up your feminine energy, and let your light shine.

7. <u>Get models</u>. Who are your role models? Think about women you admire. Who's your favorite movie star? Historical figure? Family member? Who's the happiest woman you know? The wisest? The sexiest? The most resilient? You can have different role models for different parts of life, or different parts of femininity. Ask the role models in your life how they do the great things they do. Do what they do, because it's always a good idea to take advice from successful people. Add their ideas to the ideas in this book. We are all sisters, and we are all in this together.

8. <u>Pray</u>. Whenever I walk into a room, I take a breath and send out a silent but powerful thought: If there's someone here I need to meet, let that person come to me. This puts positive energy around me, and it takes pressure off of me. Instead of swiveling my head every 30 seconds like a maniac to scan the room for eligible gen-

tlemen, I simply relax and have a good time, secure in the belief that the universe will send me what I need. Just as you don't have to scavenge for oxygen, you don't have to scavenge for men. Oxygen surrounds us, and so do men. We draw oxygen into our lungs when we inhale, and we draw men to us with a positive attitude and peaceful belief. And it works. I went to the "Harvard Comes to Chicago" alumni event where my favorite professor, Helen Vendler, was among those scheduled to speak. As I entered the room, a quick view of my surroundings told me that most of the other attendees were gentlemen who had graduated decades before I did. Although most of the people in the room had a grandfatherly look about them, I sent out my customary thought: If there's someone here I need to meet, let him come to me. Twenty seconds later, the door opened, and a handsome man in his forties walked in. He strode across the room and took a seat. Suddenly, he turned and looked at me, and he continued to glance at me during the professors' speeches. I know, because I continued to look at him too! After the talk was over, I was chatting with the woman seated on my right, and the gentleman in question marched right up to me and sat on my left. He said hello, and he asked whether he could sit with me during the luncheon portion of the event. We sat next to each other at lunch, and we chatted and flirted madly. When the lunchtime presentations began, we continued to glance at each other and grin, and I did the Shy Eye Flirt (coming soon in Chapter 6). At one point he took out a pen and began writing something. I thought, "Oh, I bet he's writing me a note." Then I thought, "Come on, Valerie, you're getting a bit too into your 8 steps. Not every man with a pen is writing you a note." But he was! The note said, "I would like to take you to dinner." He did, and we ended up dating for around three months.

Why not turn up your feminine energy every time you move from one space to another throughout your day? Turn it up when you get out of bed, and when you leave the house. Turn it up when you get on the bus. Turn it up when you get into the elevator at work. Turn it up when you go to a café for lunch, and turn it up as you step out in style for the evening. Before being concerned about being in the right place at the right time to attract the men you want to date, make sure you're in the right frame of mind. Turn up your feminine energy, and tell yourself that the man of your dreams is alive and walking the Earth and that you are attracting him with your feminine energy as if you were a planet exercising your gravitational pull. When your feminine energy is high, it means you're excited about being you. And what's more attractive than that?

To sum up Step 3, turn up your feminine energy by being excited to be a woman and excited to be you. Turn up your pink thermometer and watch that mercury rise. When you're excited about *being* you, men will get excited about *meeting* you.

Step 4

Look and Feel Your Best

Do you have an outfit that makes you feel like a million bucks the instant you put it on? The one that garners you compliments galore? That is an "A" outfit. Anything else is a "B" outfit. Now, why would you ever wear anything other than an "A" outfit? Sell, donate, or burn your B clothes, and wear only what's on the A list, even if that means wearing the same two things every day. If it doesn't make you feel great, why should you let it touch your body? (That advice applies to more than just clothes, but let's stick to talking about image for now.)

Go European

I lived in Europe for around five years, and the world agrees that European women are beautiful. Why? Because they work with what they've got, and they wear quality clothes. They don't chase after the latest trends the way some of us in the US do; rather, they dress the body that they have, and they wear colors and styles that suit their individual features, regardless of the trends. Many American women tend to buy more clothes of lesser value, favoring quantity over quality.

European women, by contrast, are more apt to spend their money on a few excellent pieces that will look good and last a long time and that they can accessorize with different scarves and jewelry. It doesn't hurt to follow the European model when dressing, meaning to look more at yourself than at the latest cover girls. What looks good on you? What suits your individual style? Create a wardrobe of A clothes, and you're telling yourself and the world that you deserve to look and feel great.

Why Bother?

You or people you know may think that paying attention to appearance is shallow or a waste of time and money. I disagree. Caring about how you look shows that you care about how you feel and how others feel. Caring about how you look shows that you are claiming your space in the world, and that you're not afraid to encourage others to notice you. Choosing not to pay attention to your appearance can be a sign of shyness or lack of social skills or lack of self-respect. Plus, don't you want to make a good impression on your future husband? Here are some reasons appearance matters:

1. <u>When you like the way you look, you like the way you feel</u>. People pick up on your comfort level with yourself. When you're confident about how you look, you can direct your energy outward and onto other people, which is where your energy belongs. When you're concerned about how you look, your energy turns inward, and you become less approachable as your feminine energy ceases to radiate out. Have you ever had a clothing stain

that you felt everyone would notice? Or a ripped hem that made you uncomfortable? Your energy then points to that stain or hem like a big red arrow, and you stop focusing on others and stop feeling confident. When you're comfortable with how you look, you send the message that you're comfortable in your skin. Now you're attracting men from a position of confidence and self-love.

2. <u>Men notice your appearance</u>. Like it or not, men are visual. Instead of ignoring or avoiding this fact, embrace it. Again, don't you want to make a great impression on your future date, future boyfriend, and future husband? My grandparents were married for 58 years, until death did them part, and my granddad Ed never got tired of telling of how pretty my grandmother Ethel looked in her yellow dress when she walked into their high school chemistry class. Chemistry indeed!

3. <u>You attract who you are</u>. When you go to a meeting, or a party, or a class, do you tend to gravitate toward people who look like you? That's a natural human tendency, and you can put it to work for you or against you. Look like a slob, and attract slobs. Look cute and trendy, and attract someone cute and trendy. Are you the athletic type? If you look sporty, chances are you'll attract someone sporty. My style happens to be classic and polished, and I attract similar men. Like attracts like, so consider this when developing your style. Look at your Man List again. Is he the tweedy professor type? An athlete? Clean cut and corporate? The odds are that your ideal style for yourself matches the style of your ideal man.

So, let your clothes help attract your dream man to you. I dress like Audrey Hepburn, and I've attracted my Cary Grant! My dream man says I'm the most stylish woman he's ever met. Style is, of course, in the eye of the beholder, and we match there too because he's the most stylish man I've ever met.

Flattery Will Get You Everywhere

Have you considered whether your clothes truly flatter you? Does your style reflect the person you are, the person you were, or the person you're becoming? Our mothers told us to dress for the next career level, and that's good advice. Why not also dress for the next life level? You can dress for the next level of confidence, fabulousness, and joy, and you'll step into that next level more quickly and confidently.

What about your figure? Certainly an attractive figure can be an asset, but an even more powerful asset is your attitude toward your figure. You can accept your figure or change it (as you can accept or change anything in your life), but either way, love yourself where you are right now. Remember, you will attract men from a position of self-love, not a position of need or unhappiness. If you're not crazy about yourself, why should anyone else be? Whether your goal is to lose, gain, or maintain your weight, get to work on it rather than complaining about it. In the meantime, wear clothes that suit the figure that you have.

On to hair and makeup: if you haven't received a compliment on your hair in more than two weeks, it's time to make some adjustments. As

Mary Kay Executive National Sales Director Gloria Mayfield Banks says, grow it, cut it, color it, or buy some more of it, but make a change, and you'll feel revitalized. Your fresh attitude will shine out, and your attitude plus your gorgeous hair will attract favorable attention. If you think men don't notice hair, ask the next man you meet.

As for your makeup, does it express a confident, beautiful you? Don't be afraid to experiment, and don't be afraid to learn new tricks. As a student and during my law career, I never wore anything but lipstick and mascara. It wasn't until I began my Mary Kay business that I learned how to do my makeup properly. Now I belong to the 50% of women in the world who won't leave home without wearing cosmetics. If clothes make the man, makeup makes the woman! Is there a culture in the world that doesn't include some form of makeup? Makeup serves many purposes, from signifying status and class, to elevating your sense of confidence and well-being.

Have you ever noticed that if you're feeling low, your mood lifts when you get up, get dressed, and get your face together? There are studies that show that female cancer patients recover better when they wear lipstick. And do you remember the scene in the movie *Thelma and Louise* in which Susan Sarandon's character, dejected and broke, sits in her car in the desert and instead of applying the lipstick that she has taken from her purse, lets it fall to the ground? Giving up lipstick represented giving up hope.

Want to know what men think of makeup? The June 2005 issue of Elle Magazine features a survey that revealed the top three things men can't stand about women's looks: unkempt body hair, sloppy clothing, and too little makeup. And, a study featured in the March 2003 issue of Oprah Winfrey's O Magazine revealed that women who wear makeup get the job faster and make 20% more money. Why? Because wearing makeup reflects self-respect, confidence, and attention to detail. Employers think that if you take care of yourself, you'll take care of the job. When you put on that lipstick, you not only boost your mood, you boost men's moods, and you boost the world's opinion of you. As Gandhi said, you must be the change you wish to see in the world. This sentiment applies to political action as well as it applies to other aspects of life such as business, personal development, dating, and beauty. Change and enhance the way you look and feel, and you change and enhance the world's response to you.

My experience has been that not only do women with a polished cosmetic look earn more, we date more too! I challenge you to make a change in your current look, whatever that look may be. When you change something, you send change outward like ripples on a pond. When you look and feel your best, you not only attract the worthy men you deserve, you might get a raise at work too! In the end, whether you opt for a fresh, natural face or a seven-layer look, make sure that your look is yours by choice, not by chance.

Whether you're a girly-girl, tomboy, or anybody in between, here are some tried-and-true appearance tips to help you take your look up a notch:

1. <u>Be memorable</u>. Someone once said that what separates us from the animals is our ability to accessorize. Wear something that stands out, such as a pin, scarf, or colorful sweater, so that you feel special and so that men can comment on it. I was once wearing a striking brooch on my lapel when a man in an elevator complimented me on it. He struck up a conversation, and we ended up dating. I know women who get positive comments on their fur coats, and a woman who gets positive feedback on her $40 thrift store coat. Whatever the memorable item is, if you feel great in it, and he can notice it, you've got a winner!

2. <u>Go barehanded</u>. Jewelry and accessories are excellent, as long as you skip the rings. A woman will instantly look at a man's hands and deduce whether he is married, allowing for not only the American style of wearing a wedding band on the third finger of the left hand, but also checking for the European custom of wearing it on the right hand. A man, however, will look at a woman's hands, and if he sees a ring on whatever finger of whatever hand, he will assume a man gave it to her. Men don't always stop to ponder the details of which finger of which hand the ring is on. You might have a jewelry box full of gorgeous rings, but success in any endeavor requires discipline. A beautiful ring on, say, the first finger of your right hand might impress other women, but it

might scare men away. Would you rather wear a fun ring now for short-term pleasure, or would you rather wear *the* ring from the man of your dreams for a lifetime?

3. <u>Manage your image always</u>. Do you ever run out of the house in pyjamas and no makeup to get the paper or walk the dog? Maybe it's Murphy's Law, but what if the man of your dreams walked by at that moment? And think to the future: If you were married, would you want your husband to see you looking grungy, or would you want to show him the gorgeous girl he married? A friend of mine often went to work in what she now describes not just as B clothes, but as C clothes, with no makeup. When I'd call her with impromptu invitations to cocktail parties or events, she'd always say that she wasn't dressed appropriately. After participating in one of my Romance Around the Corner seminars, she realized that by not looking her best she'd been missing opportunities to attract men—as well as perhaps to advance her career, and simply to feel good. Today she wears attractive clothes, makeup, and a smile, she's always ready to go, and she is attracting wonderful men!

4. <u>Show your waist</u>. Another piece of advice from your mother: don't wear baggy clothes. First, baggy clothes make you look like you're trying to hide something, and they usually end up accentuating exactly what you're trying to cover up. Secondly, it's a biological fact that men notice your hip-to-waist ratio. It doesn't always matter what size the hip and waist are, as long as the waist

goes in, the hip goes out, and everything's in proportion. I saw a documentary on PBS involving zoologist Desmond Morris in which he showed drawings of women's figures to men around the world. Whether the men were from London or a South American tribe, they chose the same drawings as most attractive: those depicting women with a proportional hip-to-waist ratio, where the waist goes in and the hip goes out. Be confident, be proud to be a woman, turn up your feminine energy, and show that waist.

5. <u>Don't neglect your nails</u>. Are you a manicure junkie, a biter, or a nail neglecter? Your future husband might not be able to tell whether the ring on your finger is a wedding ring or a trinket from the flea market (see point #2 above and leave that ring at home!), but he will notice whether your nails are neat and clean or dirty or raggedy. I keep my nails a bit glamour-girl long. They are always painted and shiny, and men notice and comment favorably!

6. <u>Have a great handbag</u>. Your purse is another little (or huge) area that you might not think men notice, but they do. Your accessories send signals about your image. They shout to the world whether you are sporty, classic, bohemian, organized, or in perpetual and hopefully charming disarray. There's no right or wrong; simply be aware that men are listening to what your purse communicates. Your handbag can also be a great conversation starter. I've had men approach me because of my purse, and I was surprised until I realized that men do look at more than what I thought they looked at. One man came up to me at a party at Chicago's Museum of

Contemporary Art and told me he liked my orange patent leather bag with bamboo handles. We ended up dating for a couple of months. Another man struck up a conversation with me at a business networking event at Chicago's Peggy Notebaert Nature Museum because he liked my white quilted bag with chain strap. He proposed dinner while leaning over my shoulder in the butterfly exhibit, which was very romantic of him, but his wedding ring didn't kindle the same feeling in me. Even so, an eye-catching purse can definitely add to your life's rich pageant.

7. <u>Wear great underwear</u>. Didn't your mother always tell you to wear clean underwear in case you were in an accident? I encourage you to wear great underwear for a different reason, though perhaps not the one you might think. While you're getting rid of your B clothes, throw out your B underwear too. Wear only underwear that makes you feel special—not because anyone but you will necessarily see it, but because it makes you feel beautiful and because you deserve it. Would you wear tattered, hole-infested, broken-elastic clothing on the outside? (If you answered yes, read this chapter again.) You don't deserve anything raggedy. You deserve to feel sexy and feminine, and when you do, your inner feeling will shine out.

8. <u>Love the way you look, and he will too</u>. Men are attracted to women who are comfortable in their own skin. When you like the way you look and feel, you're not preoccupied with details of whether your jeans make you look fat. You're so busy having a

great time being you and doing the things that you do, that men will notice.

Of course, no amount of gorgeous clothes, perfectly styled hair, or lip gloss will make up for a nasty personality, so make sure your beautiful image starts from within. If you have a pleasing and open personality, men will be attracted to you. When your vibe is working from following the 8 steps, the right men will find you, and they won't even care if your skirt is on inside out and you have broccoli in your teeth. They'll be too dazzled by your inner style to notice.

Other important components to looking and feeling your best are getting enough sleep, eating right, and exercising. I know I sound like your mother again, but these basics of healthy living really work. When you're overtired, you neither look nor feel your best, you probably won't make the best decisions or have the most positive attitude, and your stress levels might not leave you with the resources to turn up your feminine energy. Plus, exercising gives you energy, as does healthy eating, and you need that energy in order to shine and be your best you so that you'll attract the wonderful men you deserve. Try Pilates; try something; find what you like. And, fruit and vegetables are your friends; partially hydrogenated oils and white flour are not. Eat great, feel great.

I can hear you saying that your job, family, and/or other commitments leave you precious little time for sleeping, exercising, eating right, dating, or even reading this book. My life used to be like that when I was a burnt-out, overworked attorney, so I understand how you feel. I worked at a law firm that was the kind of place where if you didn't show up on Saturday, you shouldn't bother showing up on Sunday. Once I found out on a Thursday afternoon that I needed emergency surgery the next morning. Twenty-hour work days can exacerbate any health problem. I stumbled back to the office to tell the news to the partner I was working with. He said, and I quote, "hrrmmph." I took Friday off to have the surgery, and I took the weekend off to recover from the general anesthetic. When I returned to the office on Monday, the partner chewed me out for forgetting to change my outgoing voicemail message to let people know that I wouldn't be checking messages. I told him in all honesty that I was so overwhelmed by the fact of the surgery that I forgot to change my outgoing voicemail. He said, "Next time you won't." I thought to myself, "There will be no next time because I'm getting out of here before this place kills me." Another time, while working at the same firm, I went out on a date with a nice young man with whom I had rescheduled over and over again because I was on another project that kept me working twenty-hour days. I felt terrible about rescheduling, so I finally did go out with him, but I was so exhausted that I fell asleep in the restaurant! You won't be surprised to learn that there was no second date.

If you're short on time and long on stress the way I used to be, do you want your life to be like that forever? Are you using your demanding job as an excuse for not dating or attracting men? Is George Clooney or Denzel Washington going to appear at your cubicle and whisk you away to a life of happiness? Obviously, you've got to take control of your situation and find a way to magnify and multiply your own happiness. If you don't make changes, you'll continue to get the same results. The good thing is that the 8-step Romance Around the Corner plan is fun. Dating doesn't have to be hard or scary. In fact, what is scarier: making a change in your life now, or the thought of living exactly the same life five years from now? If that thought doesn't shake you out of your seat, well, check back in five years.

To sum up Step 4, you want to look and feel your best because you deserve it, and because you'll make a great impression on the men around you. Take your appearance up a notch, take your health up a notch, and watch how many notches your self-esteem rises. Watch, too, how many more dates you get, and with high-caliber men.

Step 5

Leave Your House

OK, you're feeling positive, you're raising your deserve level, you're reading your Man List, you're using the power of your subconscious mind, your feminine energy is on high, and you look and feel fantastic. The man of your dreams exists, and although you may not yet know where he is, you know where he isn't: your house. He's not sitting on your living room sofa, nor is he hiding behind the shower curtain. He's not at your place, so get out of there. To attract him, you need the right mindset, and it does help to be where he is, not where he isn't.

So where is he? That depends on who he is. Go back to your Man List and look at it strategically. To catch a thief, think like a thief. To attract your man, think like him. Is the man of your dreams an intellectual? He might be at bookstores, book fairs, gallery openings, the symphony, university lectures, children's tutoring programs, charity events, or simply the bank or church or your local drugstore or coffee shop. Is your dream man the outdoorsy type? Look for him in nature clubs, park district activities, running clubs, corporate athletic events, ski groups, volunteer children's sports programs, the country club, sporting goods stores, or simply the bank or church or your local drugstore or coffee shop. You get the idea. The point is to get out and get going. If you've got the 8 steps working for you, he'll find you.

Here are ideas on how to maximize the time spent out of your house:

1. <u>Mother knows best</u>. Follow your mother's advice to do the things you like to do so that you'll meet like-minded people. Take that scuba or guitar class you've always wanted to take. Go to charity balls for organizations you believe in, or volunteer for the campaign of your favorite candidate. If you're a sports fan, go to the game, have a hot dog, and have fun. Do things you enjoy, so that even if you don't meet anyone on that particular day, you'll still have a great time.

2. <u>Go out with girlfriends</u>. If you don't have any, go out alone and make some! Find like-minded girlfriends, and support each other in your mission to go out and attract great men. When you arrange to go out with a friend, you'll stick to it. If you feel tired after work, you'll go out anyway because you don't want to let your friend down. And whether you meet a man or not, you'll have a great time out with your girlfriend.

3. <u>Go out alone</u>. While it's good to go out with "power partners"— girlfriends who will keep you on track—it's a great idea to go out alone sometimes. It can take courage to go out alone, but fortune favors the bold! Plus, going out alone is a huge confidence

booster. Just think: If you can do that, you can do other things that involve stepping out of your comfort zone, and you'll be stronger for it. Once a friend couldn't make it to an after-work party we had planned to attend. I had already bought my ticket, and I wasn't going to let it go to waste, so, with a bit of trepidation, I showed up alone. I was mobbed! I went to the bar to order a cranberry juice, and a couple of men started talking to me. Another man who was alone joined in, and pretty soon all of the men at the party wanted to talk to the girl that all of the other men were talking to. One man insisted he have his photo taken with me, and two others asked for my phone number. I ended up going out with both of them—separately, of course—and dating one of them, who gave me a charming Valentine's Day gift of a chocolate shoe filled with chocolates.

4. <u>Go in fun, not desperation</u>. Men can smell desperation. Being desperate puts you in a position of neediness, rather than completeness, and you will attract from a position of completeness. Whether you're sweet 16, 25, 35, thirty-through, "of a certain age," young at heart, or anywhere at all on the age spectrum, go out with the attitude that you're there to have fun, to learn, and to add your sparkle to the world, not to snare a man. Isn't it an interesting phenomenon that sometimes to attract something, you can't "try" to attract it; you have to let it come to you. When you're out and about having fun, learning, sparkling, and letting the 8 steps work for you, the men on your Man List will find you.

Don't let them catch a whiff of desperation, as this will push them away. Aren't you attracted to confident men rather than needy ones? A confident man likes a confident woman. Tell yourself that you're the prize, and that the man who earns you will be a lucky man indeed.

5. <u>Do lunch</u>. Take your lunch hour (you can do it!) and go where he's likely to be, whether it's the deli or the Ritz. When I worked at the law firm, I realized that women tended to work through lunch more than men. It might be different where you work, but I'll bet that when you step out at lunchtime, you find packs of men, and men in ones and twos. The man of your dreams just might be out for a bite to eat tomorrow at lunchtime, and you won't meet him if you're sitting at your desk. Even if you bring a lunch to work, pop out for a 15 minute walk, or run a few errands, or dash into the local bookstore to browse the titles—and the aisles—for a few minutes. The title of this chapter is Leave Your House, and that means Leave Your Office, too. Of course, you just might find wonderful men at the office. Office romances have been the subject of movies, books, and tabloid sensationalism, so use your best judgment and set your priorities. The 8 steps are based on sticking to what's tried-and-true and not getting caught up worrying about exceptions to the rule. One tried-and-true statement is be careful, while another is love is where you find it.

6. <u>Make a schedule</u>. It's been said that most people plan their vacations better than they plan their lives. It's also true that many peo-

ple are more organized at work than in their personal lives. If your social and romantic life is going great without a plan, congratulations. If on the other hand you'd like to see some improvements, you're going to want to change something. If you're searching for a new condo, you set specific times to work with your real estate agent to look at different properties. Why not be equally organized in attracting dates? Make a schedule. How many nights a week are you willing to go out, even if it's just for a walk or to the drugstore? How many times a week will you go outside at lunchtime? And don't tell me you don't feel like it. There's no time for excuses; the man of your dreams is waiting for you. You don't always feel like going to work, do you? But you show up at the office anyway, and you get a paycheck. Show up in the world with your 8 steps, and you'll get dates.

7. <u>Let no one rain on your parade</u>. If friends or family members scoff at your practice of the 8 steps, do what my mother always recommended: consider the source. Anyone who pours negativity on your dating goals probably isn't a model of dating prowess herself. Anyone who would rain on your parade probably doesn't have one of her own. I always knew that I didn't know it all, but I knew enough to take advice from successful people. Run from negative people, and keep shining.

8. <u>Hang in there</u>. Don't grow discouraged if you don't meet your dream man or get a date on your first outing to the ballpark, bookstore, or bank. Roses don't grow overnight. What if the next party

you *don't* go to is the party your dream man *does* go to? Or what if there's a woman at that party who could introduce you to your dream man, or invite you to the event that will lead you to your dream man? Have you heard of six degrees of separation? The idea is that each of us knows someone who knows someone else, etc., and that each of us is just six people away from any one else. You are just six people away from the man of your dreams. Keep doing the things you know you need to do, like leaving your house, and the results will come. I didn't meet my dream man the first time I started putting together the 8 steps. I didn't meet him the first year. But I did meet wonderful and interesting and challenging and exciting and kind men along the way. I had good dates and bad ones and disastrous ones that can be spoken of only after everyone is dead. But I didn't quit. What if I gave up before meeting the man of my dreams? Perish the thought! Keep going, because sometimes miracles wait to appear until what seems like the 11th hour. Romance is around the corner.

Divide and Conquer

It's fun to go out with girlfriends, and setting up a night out with the girls is important because you're more likely to stick to the schedule and actually leave your house if you've already committed to your friends. Plus, your friends might have invitations to different parties, or have additional ideas on where to go. So, team up and cover more territory.

Make sure, though, that when you go out with girlfriends, you're not joined at the hip. You don't want to be an impenetrable clump of women that no man dares approach. Of course, some men will march right up to you no matter how many other women surround you—I've had men approach me when I'm out with other *men*!—but many men will not come up to you if you're with a lot of girlfriends. Split off from the girl pack, and you'll give men an opportunity to come up to you and say hello. You can always rejoin your group of girlfriends to compare notes later.

I was at a gallery opening with a girlfriend, and we decided I'd go get some sparkling water at the bar while she checked out the hors-d'oevres. As I approached the bar, a tall, dark, and handsome man approached me. Just as we talked about not using your busy job as an excuse not to go out, don't use your girlfriends as security blankets when you do go out. Break off, stride with purpose, stand with confidence, and attract purposeful, confident men.

You Don't Have Time Not To

Are you thinking about how much time it will take to go out to events, about how your schedule is too full for this, and about all the other reasons it won't work? Turn your thinking around if you want to turn your experience around. You don't have time *not* to go out. What are your priorities? Instead of prioritizing your schedule, schedule your priorities. Think about how wonderful you'll feel if you have an exciting dating life. Bask in the thought of it. Decide to make it happen. No goal is too lofty if you're willing to do the work. Old habits are hard to break, and if you're in the habit of going from home to the office to home to the office, it will take a conscious decision to break that habit. Replace it with the habit of taking a walk before you go home. Or going out for lunch instead of eating at your desk. Or going out with girlfriends two to four nights a week. Give up TV, give up scrubbing the tub, get a housekeeper, and use that time to leave your house. Once you replace your shut-in habit with a go-out habit, that habit will be hard to break, too. Success and failure are habits. Don't fret; just start where you are. Action works better than tears. You took action in picking up this book. Congratulations! See it through. Get into the habit of a fun and successful dating life, and you'll be thrilled that you did.

Know too that once you form the habit of doing the internal work in this book—turning up your feminine energy, writing and studying your Man List, raising your deserve level, etc.—practicing the 8 steps doesn't have to take as much time out of your day as you think. It takes 21 days to form a habit, and once you do, the habit flows into your life. We don't think of the time we spend breathing; we breathe in the background of our life, and we're glad we do. Doing your internal work will become like breathing. It will weave through your life, and you'll love the results so much that you'll be glad you took the time to form habits that will set your life on your chosen path—the path along which your dream man will run to gather you in his arms.

To sum up Step 5, the man of your dreams is somewhere out there; he's not at your place. So leave your house! Go out with girlfriends, and go out alone. Make sure that your attitude is positive rather than desperate, and make a schedule so that you'll stick to a plan of leaving your house. Be in the right frame of mind, and he'll find you—but only if you're somewhere you can be found.

Step 6

Flirt, Flirt, Flirt!

Flirting is becoming a lost art in America. We are going to revive it, because it works! Put flirting to work for you, and you'll have more fun, feel better about yourself, and get more dates. What is flirting, and what isn't it? It's not throwing yourself at a man. It's not sticking to him like a bad suit. It's not being phony or plastic or someone you're not. Flirting is showing in a fun, lighthearted way that you notice the other person. Flirting shows that you're comfortable with who you are and confident enough to put attention on the other person. Flirting is playful, healthy, and doesn't have to lead to anything more than a smile. Flirting makes everyone come away feeling good. I flirted with the man of my dreams when we first met, and I still do. Flirting doesn't stop once you're dating, or once you're married. Flirting is sincere. Flirting in a relationship is a sign of love. Flirting keeps the fires burning!

How to flirt? It's easy! Here are four great ways to do it:

1. <u>The Shy Eye Flirt</u>. Finally, we're covering the fabulous Shy Eye Flirt! This simple, natural activity is something that many women do instinctively, and it drives men to distraction, fits of excitement, and the inability to refrain from asking for your phone number. Whether you're a natural flirt or a learned flirt, the Shy Eye Flirt is about to become your best friend. It's simple: look at him, look down, look up again, then down again. Wear a gentle smile. Does it sound too simple to be effective? Try it, and be astounded. Remember lovely Princess Diana, known as Shy Di, and how she'd peek up diagonally under her bangs? That's it! Do it, and men will go wild. And here's the best part: When he approaches you after you do the Shy Eye Flirt, he'll think he made the first move. Men love the chase, so let them chase you. Practice this one ten times daily, and you'll be a pro. Tip: make sure that you look down, not away, so that you don't break the magic. Here's one of my favorite Shy Eye experiences: Once I was on the train coming in from the airport, and I noticed a cute young man sitting a few seats away. When I say young, I mean younger than I am. I tend to be attracted to older men, but it's good to exercise your flirting muscles, and he was cute after all, so I looked up at him out of the corner of my eyes, let the corners of my lips turn up ever so slowly and slightly, looked down, looked back up, and looked down again. I could see a pulse of excitement surge through him as he smiled back. So, I did the Shy Eye Flirt again. He got even more excited! Then, I focused on not missing my train stop. As I stood up to get off of the train, I noticed that he

was writing something down. I thought, "Oh, I bet he's writing me a note!" Then I thought, "Come on, Valerie, you might be getting a bit too into your 8 steps. Not every man with a pen is writing you a note." But he was! I started to think afterward that maybe every man with a pen *is* writing me a note. In any case, our cute young man stood up, and before the doors of the train opened, he handed me a golden American Express envelope. I thought, "Good heavens, is he giving me money?" I smiled and took the envelope and said thank you, he smiled back, and I stepped off the train. He stayed on, the doors closed, and the train rolled away. I opened the envelope immediately—there was no American Express gift certificate inside, but there was a note that had "Yours To Enjoy" printed at the top, presumably so that the gift certificate giver could write a note to the recipient. Our young man had written, "I couldn't help but notice a beautiful woman riding alone on the train. If you ever need some company, I'll be 'yours to enjoy.'" He signed it and added his phone number. Well, anyone who writes a note like that deserves a call, wouldn't you agree? I called him the next day, and we went out soon thereafter and had a blast. He was a gentle and brilliant man of 28, and I was 33. We had some wonderful dates before deciding that we were simply on different paths at these stages of our lives. I do remember that on our first date he looked at my hands and asked why a woman like me didn't have any wedding rings. Men do notice your hands; see Chapter 4.

2. <u>The Drive-By Flirt</u>. This is fun, and it elicits the chase! If you're at a party, and you see someone interesting, you can walk by, make a comment, and keep going. For example, you might comment on the environment by saying, "This party is full of interesting people, isn't it?" and just keep walking. If he wants to follow you, he will. The Drive-By Flirt is great because it establishes you as someone who's confident rather than needy, and it lets him engage in hot pursuit as he's in danger of losing you in the crowd.

3. <u>The Conversational Flirt</u>. If a gentleman begins conversation with you, do you freeze up and get tongue-tied, which is what I used to do? Once a guy I had a crush on in college actually said hello to me. I was so unprepared that I squinched my face up into a largely indescribable yet definitely bizarre expression, and he never spoke to me again. Or are you someone who slips easily into witty banter like Katharine Hepburn in the movies? At the very least, you want to be interested and interesting. Simply be positive, ask questions, and throw in the Shy Eye Flirt for good measure. Don't forget to breathe. Does that sound funny? When we get tense, our breathing often becomes strained. It works both ways: if we make a conscious effort to breathe deeply, we become more relaxed. And, more oxygen to the brain means we'll think more clearly and engage in conversational flirting more easily. Simply talk about your environment, ask open-ended questions about his work and his life, and be lighthearted. Flirting isn't about being serious; it's about having fun.

4. <u>The Practice Flirt</u>. Opportunities to flirt surround us if we open our eyes and look around. Flirting is natural, fat-free, non-caloric, and good for the physical and mental health of both parties. You can practice your Shy Eye Flirt from across a coffee shop. You can practice your Conversational Flirt or Drive-By Flirt at the grocery store. It's ok if you're madly in love with the person you're flirting with; it's also ok to flirt with someone you don't want to date. You're just engaging in a positive interaction. That's another way of saying that flirting can be a quick exchange that leads to nothing more, and that makes both people feel better about themselves. Everybody wins! Practice flirting every day, and when it's time for a flirt that really matters, you'll be ready! Champions are not made in the ring; they're made in their daily practice, and the ring is simply where they are recognized. I was in line at the grocery store one day, and I noticed a man get in line behind me. He didn't look like my type, but I told myself it never hurts to practice flirt. So, I turned around and gave him the Shy Eye. It worked! The next thing I knew, he tapped me on the shoulder. I turned around again, and he told me he was visiting Chicago and asked whether I knew any fun things to do. What a golden opportunity to have turned that into a date if that's what I had wanted! I could have said, "In fact, I'm going to a club tonight. Do you like clubs?" I didn't want to go out with him, though, so I said, "In fact, we're right by Navy Pier. I bet you'll love the sights and shops and exhibits." We continued chatting, and I paid for my groceries. As I picked up my grocery bag and started to leave, I

· gave him a big smile and told him I hoped he'd enjoy his stay in Chicago. He felt happy, I felt happy, and maybe he met the girl of his dreams on Navy Pier!

To sum up Step 6, fall in love with flirting! Flirting is simply a fun, lighthearted way to let the other person know you noticed him. You can flirt with words, with a smile, or simply with your eyes. Practice the Shy Eye Flirt by peeking up at a man, looking down, and then looking back up again. This small activity drives men wild and lets them begin the chase. Admit it: They love to chase us, and we love to be chased! Flirting simply initiates and furthers that age-old yet always modern dance.

Step 7

You've Got a Date! Now What?

Hooray! You've got a date! What to do now? The short answer is: keep flirting. You want to dazzle him, discover him, check for deal breakers, and of course have fun in the process. You'll dazzle him simply by showing him the fabulous creature that you are. You'll discover him as you find out about him, learn what makes him special, and decide whether he is worthy of you. Checking your dealbreakers means finding out if there are any deep incompatibilities so that you know sooner rather than later whether you're wasting your time. And you'll have fun because no matter how bad the date might be, you're going to be polite and cheerful. After all, someone at the next table might be the man for you! And if it's a good date, you'll maximize your fun to have a truly great time.

Let's walk through a date from what to wear and what to say, to how to end the evening, starting with how to dazzle him:

1. <u>Your appearance</u>. Wear something that makes you look and feel your best, and something that is appropriate to the occasion. One of my Romance Around the Corner seminar clients in New York advises taking a bubble bath to feel relaxed and luxurious before you go out. After you're pampered and happy, choose a flattering outfit. Bright colors can be very attractive, and they show confidence. Feel great about your clothes, hair, and makeup, and your happiness will radiate out. Right before a date is not the time to experiment for the first time with home hair coloring or liquid eyeliner. Stick to what you know works for you. Tip: don't forget the lip gloss. Men like a glossy lip.

2. <u>Accept his compliment</u>. Your date might tell you how nice you look. Resist any urge to say, "this old thing?" or "you look great too." The proper response to a compliment is, "thank you!" This shows that you are confident, that you agree that you look wonderful, and that you appreciate his noticing how exquisite you look. Bask in the compliment, and you'll probably receive more of them.

3. <u>Tell positive anecdotes</u>. Prepare some happy little stories in advance such as bits about something funny and upbeat that happened that day, or a great movie you saw, or why you love living in your city. Stay away from complaining about your job, your dating life, your ex-boyfriend, your ex-husband, your sciatica, your roommate, or anything else. Avoid stories of doom and gloom. Put your best foot forward and your best attitude forward.

Everyone knows (or should know) that the other person wants to show his or her best side on a date. If your best side involves crankiness, that won't bode well for your other sides. Have you ever been on a date with someone who grumbled the whole time about his job, griped about his boss, was mean to the waitress, complained about the table at the restaurant, sent the food back, and never once asked you anything about yourself? I have, and it didn't inspire the urge for a second date.

4. <u>Let your body language do some talking</u>. Sit with open body language, so that you look comfortable and interested, instead of nervous and like you'd rather be at the dentist. A cocked head signals interest, so tilt your head when he says something interesting. Keep a gentle smile on your lips. Sit with good posture, with your hands open, and lean in slightly. This kind of body language will tell him that you're confident enough in your own skin to open up to someone else. Plus, when you sit with confident and comfortable body language, you'll actually feel confident and comfortable! Did you know that studies show that people judge us based only 7% on the content of what we say? The other 93% of judgment is based on the tone of our voice and on our body language.

5. <u>Modulate</u>. Speaking of the tone of your voice, what's it like? Do you sound rushed and nervous? Are you squeaky and breathy with anxiety? Breathe deeply, speak from the diaphragm, and put a little bit of inflection into your voice to create interest. Have you heard the old joke about the newscaster who had a face made for

radio? Don't have a voice made for print media. If you like, take a tip from Daisy Buchanan in The Great Gatsby, whom the narrator suspects lowers her voice intentionally to make her listener lean into her. Just be aware of your voice, and your voice will be great.

6. Touch his arm. If you like him, touch his arm. There's no need for gripping or grabbing; just give his arm a light touch as you laugh or say something. Touching his arm will signal that you like him, and believe me, he will pick up on that signal if he is not in a coma. Have you ever noticed that a simple arm touch makes a man feel great? Try it and see.

7. Do the Shy Eye Flirt. The Shy Eye Flirt (see Chapter 6) works everywhere and anywhere, and it is particularly enhanced by candlelight. Flirting isn't simply a way to get a date, it's a way to get a second date. It's a way to have a happy relationship with a boyfriend. It's a way to keep things fun and sexy with your husband. It's a way of life! Don't forget to flirt flirt flirt while on the date.

8. Do what got you there. Keep being the wonderful person you were when he met you and asked you out. Our mothers' advice to "be yourself" is very wise. Of course, if being yourself means being cranky, sullen, or morose, knock it off. Revisit Step 1 of this book and love yourself. Negative characteristics come from low self-esteem and from pain. Keep working the 8 steps to raise your self-esteem, to heal yourself, and to enjoy your journey. Being the true

you means being a wonderful you. So be yourself, and he'll be dazzled. Doesn't it always seem to turn out that Mom was right?

While you're dazzling him, discover him. Here's how:

1. <u>Ask</u>. Wouldn't you agree that the best way to find out something is to ask? Ask your date open-ended questions, and be interested in the answers. Some great questions are, "What are your favorite things to do around town?" "Where are you planning to travel next?" "What are you reading these days?" A gentle and conversational way to ask questions can be to preface them with a statement. For example, you might say, "I just saw the movie *Million Dollar Baby* and thought it had some really interesting themes. What good movies have you seen lately?"

2. <u>Don't interrogate</u>. Remember that while asking questions is good, a date is not a senate committee hearing or a police interrogation scene. Giving your date the third degree will likely turn him off. A man doesn't want to think you're ticking off a questionnaire, or that you're interviewing him for marriage compatibility on the first date. Interrogating him makes you seem desperate to find Mr. Right, and it takes the fun right out of the date. A good rule of thumb in dating—and in life—is to put yourself in the other persons' shoes. If your date fired a barrage of questions at you about your family history, medical records, earning potential, fertility, credit reports, and college transcripts, how would you feel? But if

he asked kindhearted questions that showed genuine interest in who you are and what you're about, wouldn't you be flattered?

Let's continue walking through the date. You're dazzling him, you're discovering him, and you also want to find out if there are any dealbreakers. Dealbreakers are insurmountable incompatibilities, and here's how to find out if your date is triggering them:

1. <u>Know your dealbreakers</u>. You've made your Man List to clarify what you want in a man. What *don't* you want in a man? What can you absolutely not tolerate? What makes someone utterly incompatible with you? You might have a dealbreaker on your hands if he wants a suburban lifestyle while you're a city girl through and through. Or, if you're highly extroverted and he's highly introverted, that might be a dealbreaker. Of course, one woman's dealbreaker might be another woman's compromise. There's no right or wrong; it's just a question of knowing what you want and what you don't. I read that the rabbi who started speed dating sessions for his congregation did so because he'd noticed in years of couples counseling that some couples had deep incompatibilities that could have been discovered early on, before the couple dated for months or stayed married for years. Save yourself lots of heartache down the road by checking your dealbreakers at the beginning.

2. <u>Ask gentle questions</u>. By letting him talk and reveal himself in areas where you know dealbreakers might lurk, you'll have the chance to discover any dealbreakers without sliding a question-

naire across the table to him. For example, you might ask, "If you had a day you could spend however you wanted, what would be your perfect day?" This might reveal his preferred lifestyle, and you can keep your ears open for dealbreakers. Or, if differences in spirituality and religion might be a dealbreaker for you, you might say something like, "I found a great church in town; are you a churchgoer?" A great way to find out his priorities would be to ask, "You seem to have such a wonderfully full life; how do you do it all?" or, "Someone once asked me what I would recommend if a rich aunt had $5 million to give away, but not to me. If she were your aunt, which organizations would you tell her to give the money to?" And you might want to recall that classic question, "So are you married?"

3. <u>Stay out of danger</u>. Anyone who is rude, condescending, or threatening to you has obviously tripped the dealbreaker alarm. You deserve someone who treats you like a queen. If you're in danger, call security. Call 911. Get out of there!

4. <u>Let him ask too</u>. He might be trying to find out if you hit any of *his* dealbreakers. Back when I was using a matchmaking service, I was once on a date with a fellow who was very nice but who instantly tripped dealbreaker alarms with me, and vice versa. I knew there was trouble before we even went on the date, because on the phone, we had no spark. Still, we kept talking, and he asked me where I wanted to meet. I'm a bit old-fashioned and love it when the man decides, but I'm willing to give modern men a try,

and I'm always prepared with a restaurant or movie suggestion when asked. So, I suggested this little French café, and he said no. He said he wanted to go to a particular Italian restaurant. Against my better judgment, I didn't call the whole thing off right then and there. I said fine, and on the day of our date I hopped in a taxi and headed toward the Italian restaurant. He called me on my cell phone while I was in the taxi and said he meant a different restaurant; another Italian restaurant that was around the corner from the first one. I found the situation a bit odd but said ok. I'd never been to the second restaurant before, and as soon as I walked in, I realized that while my outfit was perfect for the first one, I was a bit overdressed for the second one. Have you ever seen a movie or TV show or commercial where a character walks into a room, the jukebox screeches to a halt, and everyone stops conversing, stops eating, freezes, and stares? That's how I felt when, wearing diamonds and high heels and a lovely and dramatic wrap pinned with a diamond and pearl brooch, I swept into a blue collar, family-style pizzeria with peanut shells on the floor, sports jerseys and beer posters on the wall, and an actual jukebox. I never let little things bother me, so I ignored the stares, gave the room a gentle smile, and found my date in a booth in the back. The matchmaking service was one that didn't give you photos of your date in advance, and my date turned out not to fit at all the tall, dark, and handsome physical description I had told the matchmaking service I favor. I somehow got the impression from the look on his face that I was way off from his preferred physical type, too. I would have matched him with the girl-next-door type, which I really am not, unless you live in a very specific neighborhood. In any case, we started chatting, and I asked him what activities he enjoyed outside of work. He said that he loved skiing and other winter sports, and asked if I ski. I told him that while I love the "après-ski" activities such as sitting by the fire at the ski lodge while wearing a warm fuzzy sweater and sipping hot chocolate, I don't ski because I have a tiny little circulatory condition that causes me to suffer terribly from the cold. (It's called Reynaud's, and if I get too cold, my arteries start to shut down. My sister has it too, so growing up we thought it was normal.) My date looked at me and said, "So you don't ski? What about sledding?" I repeated, very kindly, that because of my little circulatory situation I suffered terribly from the cold and wasn't a sledder. He asked, somewhat suspiciously, "What about outdoor ice skating?" The conversation went on like this for much too long, although the date itself was quite short. We had nothing in common except mutual dealbreakers.

This takes us right to what to do if you're on a bad date. A bad date is one where you don't like him, he doesn't like you, and you're just not clicking. Let me reiterate that if he's rude, crude, threatening, or abusive, that is not just a bad date; that is a hostile situation. Call security. Call 911. Get out of there! Dating is supposed to be a fun opportunity to dazzle, discover, and check your dealbreakers. Dating is not supposed to involve taking your life into your hands. But if we're talking about a standard bad date where there's just no chemistry and you have nothing in common, here's what to do:

1. <u>Don't panic</u>. Remain calm and resist the urge to run screaming from the building. Bad dates happen to good people; don't flip out. In fact, try to treat it as a learning experience, which is what I did on the bad date with the winter sports aficionado described above. Ask yourself, How did I get into this situation in the first place? Could I have found out more about him in advance? Did I ignore my intuition at any point? Have I learned anything that will help me update and refine my Man List or my dealbreakers list? As you fine tune your working of the 8 steps, you will have fewer and fewer bad dates. The wavelength of feminine energy that you put out will be specific to the type of man you think about, and that is the type of man who will approach you. In the meantime, don't stress out because you had a bad date, and don't take it personally. Take from it whatever knowledge you can, and blow away the chaff. Remember that to some extent, dating is a numbers game: as our mothers told us, we've got to meet some frogs before we meet our prince. This makes us appreciate the prince even more, and it builds character and resilience.

2. <u>Think business</u>. Treat a bad date like a bad business meeting: be pleasant and polite, and exit as gracefully and as soon as you can. Don't chastise or castigate the poor man, don't be mean to him, and don't shut him down. Remember the Golden Rule, and treat him the way you hope he would treat you. Also, we women are all

sisters, and we are all in this dating game together. Let your bad date keep his confidence and save face so that he will have the confidence to go out with the next woman, who just might think he's a good date or even the perfect match for her. Plus, if you are mean to your date, that handsome man at the next table might notice your bad attitude and change his mind about saying hello when you are on your way to powder your nose. Keep a bad date short; there's no need for dessert, coffee, the cheese course, or a nightcap. Go home early and get your beauty rest for the next date, which might be with your prince instead of a frog.

Let's cover a few more aspects of the date, including what to do if one or both of you had what some people affectionately call a "starter" marriage. As I've mentioned, I'm between husbands myself, and you may have dated men who are between wives. This is a fact of life, and there are ways to deal with it gracefully.

1. Be glad. Rejoice if he's divorced; it means he's probably trained. Truly, if he's in his late thirties and has never been married, don't you wonder the tiniest bit what he's been doing with his time? And if he's in his forties or fifties or any decade after that and has never been married, could this be a red flag that this man is just not going to get married? Men who used to be called "confirmed bachelors" seem today to be called "players." If you're just looking to play, be careful and safe. If you're looking for more than a fling, and you're looking for a man over 35, this might mean that you're looking for a divorced man. There are always exceptions,

but these days I'm more surprised if someone has never been married than if he's divorced. At least he gave it a try! And most people who were married once get married again. So, if you're on a date with a divorced man, chances are he's the "marrying type." And in any case he's human; judge not lest ye be judged.

2. <u>Keep it clean</u>. Resist any urge to say mean or dirty things about your ex. This only makes you look bad, and he'll think that you're bitter and hate all men. If you are bitter or do hate men, fix this! Bitterness and resentment act as weights around your ankles, keeping you from being your best. You might want to seek counseling, join a support group, keep a journal, or work more on Step 1—Love Yourself. Love, gratitude, and acceptance leave no room for bitterness and hate. Do what you need to do to get healthy, inside and out. You deserve it. Back to your date: remember that you want to dazzle him, not depress or disturb him! If your date asks questions about your ex or your divorce that go a little bit too deep for your taste, especially if you're on your first or second date, you could lightheartedly say something like, "Oh, there will be plenty of time to talk about that later. So tell me more about your work" (or your children/vacation/home remodeling project/cross country motorcycle tour). Be graceful, and grace will return to you.

3. <u>Be aware</u>. Be wary if he badmouths his ex. If he talks about his ex negatively, what would stop him from one day talking about you negatively? Do you want to date someone bitter? Do you want to

be his rebound girl? And anyway, there are two sides to every story. Notice not only how he talks about his ex, but also how he talks about his children, if he has any. Does he love them? Does he pay child support? If he's a deadbeat dad, run! Run fast! Run far!

4. <u>Skip the grill</u>. Don't grill him on the details of his divorce. If he says he's divorced, don't say, "Why? What went wrong? What on Earth did you do to her?" Just say, "Me too." or "For how long?" or "Do you have any children?" and then steer the conversation elsewhere, such as to the menu or your surroundings or the news of the day. There's plenty of time to find out more about his divorce after the first or second date. At the beginning, you simply want to discover the parameters of who he is, not learn every nitty-gritty detail of his past, see a copy of the divorce decree, or interview his children, ex-wife, and divorce attorney.

You've dazzled and discovered and checked your dealbreakers, and now it's time to go home and dream—about him, or about your dream man who's still out there, depending on how the date went. At the end of the date:

1. <u>Say thank you</u>. Remember to thank him for the evening. Men want to be appreciated too! If you had a great time, tell him. (And this is a good time to touch his arm and throw in a Shy Eye Flirt if you like him.) If you're on a traditional date and he paid, thank him for that. If you're on a "dutch" date and you split the bill, you

can still thank him for a fun time. More than one man has told me that many women don't say thank you, and that they like it when we do. Good manners are always appropriate, even on a date.

2. <u>Keep it clean</u>. No sex on the first date. You're a woman of mystery. Let him chase you, let him fantasize about you, let him earn you. Earning you takes time; it doesn't happen right after dessert. Plus, sex causes emotional attachment, and you want to be careful to whom you get attached, especially early in the game.

3. <u>Keep your dignity</u>. If he doesn't call again, don't call him. I repeat, don't call him. I repeat, *don't call him*! He has not been mugged and is not sprawled out wounded, with no cell phone, in a gutter, moaning your name. Doesn't your Man List say that you want someone who's crazy about you? If he's "not that into you," why on Earth would you be into him? If Mr. First Date doesn't call, date someone else. And be happy about it! As my mother taught me, man's rejection is God's protection. Keep your energy moving forward, keep having fun, and keep your feminine energy high. When you stay focused on your Man List and on moving forward, you will attract fewer and fewer men who are ambivalent and more and more men who are intrigued by you and who can't resist your pull.

To sum up Step 7, when you go on a date, you want to dazzle, discover, and check your dealbreakers. Show him with your style, talk, voice, and body language that you are a fabulous creature indeed. Discover who he is—not through Soviet-era police interrogation tactics—but through fun, flirty, gentle questions. Find out if any dealbreakers are in play; it's always better to find out earlier rather than later if you've got insurmountable incompatibilities. And above all, have fun and keep flirting. If you're on a bad date and you can't have fun, have a learning experience, and get ready to have fun on your next date with someone else.

Step 8

Be True To Yourself

It's been said that women who find their dream man love him, but they love themselves more. Their self-love is what allows them to hang in there, improving themselves and refusing to settle, until they attract the one whom they love and who loves them. You've raised your self-esteem and continue to do so, you've made your Man List and you know who you want, and you're working the 8 steps beautifully. Don't settle for less than what you desire and deserve, and don't compromise who you are in the process. Becoming your best is the best way to meet the best man for you!

Here's how to stay true to yourself and keep going even when the going seems tough:

1. <u>Keep your eyes on the prize</u>. Focus on your Man List and tell yourself it's just a matter of time before you attract that man to you. In fact, tell yourself that you are attracting him to you right now. Every day brings you closer to meeting him. Remember why

you want what you do. How will you feel when you're dating a wonderful man? Feel that way right now. Paint a positive picture and step into it.

2. <u>Get some power partners</u>. Go out with like-minded girlfriends. Keep each others' spirits high. Don't let each other fall. A journal can be a great power partner too; writing down your thoughts and experiences helps you make sense of them, helps you see patterns, helps you work through problems, and helps you see progress. Do what makes you stronger.

3. <u>Consistency is key</u>. If you turn your feminine energy up only once a week, you're letting possibly compatible men pass you by six days out of seven. If you work on raising your self-esteem only once in a while, you might find you're taking one step forward and two steps back. Follow the plan every day, and follow all 8 steps. It takes 21 days to form a habit, and it's hard to break it once you form it. So, keep forming good habits because habits create character—and character creates destiny.

4. <u>Give up to go up</u>. What can you eliminate from your life that is holding you back? Do you come home from work and zonk out in front of the TV for three hours before collapsing into bed and dragging yourself up in the morning to do it all over again? Do you spend hours gossiping with negative friends? Do you have addictions or compulsions that interfere with your life? Give up what is extraneous or harmful and watch your energy go up, watch your free time go up, watch your positivity go up. When

you give something up, though, be sure to fill that void with something positive, or else the negative thing could creep back in. One reason that we sometimes fail in our attempts to give up bad eating habits, smoking, or other addictions is that we fail to replace the negative habit with a positive one. Nature abhors a vacuum, and if you take something away, something will replace it. Fill that space with something positive; fill it with the 8 steps!

5. <u>Stay positive</u>. Feed your mind positive books, CDs, movies, affirmations, and conversations. And let no one rain on your parade. People who try to do that are in pain because they don't have a parade of their own. If someone is mean to you, it's because she's hurting and doesn't have enough love in her life. Pray for her, and move on. You know your value, and you know your mission. Anyone who disagrees can just get out of the way while you live your fabulous life!

6. <u>Relax</u>. Don't worry if the universe's time frame isn't your time frame. Patience is truly a virtue. Keep doing what you know you should do, and you will see results. If you're struggling with the idea that you want to find a man so that you can have a family before your biological clock ticks out, I want you to set that worry down, as difficult as that may seem. Don't set the goal down; set the worry down. Keep your dream and let it be an engine of joy, not stress. What if instead of telling yourself that there isn't enough time, you told yourself that your possibilities are expanding every day? Perhaps it's counterintuitive, but sometimes if you

struggle and strain, you push your goal away from you. Have you ever tried to get a cat to come over to you? The more you coax that cat, the deeper it hides under the bookshelf. But when you turn away, and start writing a letter or fixing a sandwich or checking your email, there's that cat, winding around your leg for attention and affection. Live your life, and good things will find you. Chase them, and you might chase them away.

7. <u>Don't worry; be happy</u>. Similarly, by worrying about what you don't have, you focus on what you lack. What you focus on, you magnify and multiply. Focus on lack, and create more lack. Focus on not enough time, and time ticks even faster. So don't focus on a lack of dates, focus on the idea that romance is around the corner! Things will work out, though not always the way we expect they will. For instance, when I was looking around for a new career, I wanted something creative, glamorous, and lucrative, where I could set my own hours and be the boss. I never imagined that Mary Kay would offer me all of that, and that I'd become a "Mary Kay lady." I was a Harvard-educated lawyer, and frankly I thought "peddling" lipstick was beneath me. What I didn't know was that Mary Kay is one of the most sophisticated companies on Earth. I didn't know that the sales side of the business involves corporate pampering sessions, Internet sales, and generally helping women look and feel beautiful. I didn't know that there was a leadership side to the business, through which my role is to empower other women in business. I didn't know about the annu-

al Seminars, featuring ballgowns, diamonds, and applause. I didn't know that Mary Kay's mission is to enrich women's lives. In other words, I found what I was looking for in a career; I simply didn't expect it to have a big pink ribbon tied around it! I used to worry that I was trapped in my law job and that I'd never find my way out. I then realized that my attitude would be the key to success or the lock on the door. Worry and you attract worry. Be positive, and you attract positive people, positive circumstances, and positive results. Truly, has worry ever taken you where you wanted to go? Or have you found that when you let go, the solution comes? Sometimes in preparing a speech or an article, I'll get stuck and frustrated. I'll hammer away at the problem, and that will only make it worse. So, I'll set down what I'm working on, make a cup of tea, and read a book that has absolutely nothing to do with what I'm working on. Somehow, this will free up my mind, and the answer will come to me. To begin letting go of worry, sweep it into a mental box, and tell yourself you can take it out of the box only at certain times. It'll be there when you want it! And in time, you might find that that box is just taking up space that you could be using for something more productive, and that you're ready to get rid of worry once and for all. Replace your worry with positive expectation, belief, and action, and you're on your way.

8. <u>Enjoy the journey</u>. We are on Earth to reach toward our potential, and to help others do the same. You are not only on a mission to

attract the man of your dreams—wonderful as that is—but you also are on a mission of self-discovery and growth. Have you heard the phrase, "Life is what happens while you're making other plans?" Don't fall into that trap! Don't miss life! Live before you die. Tomorrow isn't promised to us, so let's enjoy today. It's been said that if you can laugh at yourself, you'll never run out of amusing material. It's also been said that if you hold laughter in, your hips grow. Take the lesson, leave the experience, and never let yourself become frustrated at any point along your journey. No snowflake falls in the wrong place. The universe is unfolding as it should. You are on your right path. Romance is around the corner, in your heart, and in the very fabric of the air. Evolve, grow, and have fun in the process!

Step 8 will take you full-circle. To sum it up: never settle. Never give up, never compromise your integrity, never stop laughing, and never stop dreaming. You will attract a man who is worthy of you only if you stay true to yourself. And you will stay true to yourself by leaving worry behind, leaving negative habits behind, and growing into the person you were meant to be. Keep working the 8 steps, and watch previously undreamed of magic, beauty, and love fill your life.

Conclusion

All champions have in common the decision to be a champion. Decide to be your best you. Decide to have a thrilling and satisfying dating life. Decide to enjoy your journey. Decide to raise your expectation and belief to new heights. Decide to attract the man of your dreams. Decide to follow the 8 steps and to incorporate them into your day and your life. Decide and then act!

Here are the 8 steps in one place for you:

Step 1   <u>Love Yourself</u>
Raise your self-esteem and raise your deserve level. Be your best you, and you'll attract the best man for you.

Step 2   <u>Know Who You Want, and Program Your Subconscious Mind to Attract Him</u>
Make your Man List, and read it every morning and every night. Tell yourself that the man on this list is alive and walking the Earth, and that you are attracting him to you like a magnet.

Step 3   **Turn Up Your Feminine Energy**
          Be excited to be a woman, and let your feminine energy flow.

Step 4   **Look and Feel Your Best**
          Manage your appearance all the time. Throw out your B clothes and wear only the A outfits. Put pep in your step and a smile on your face. Confidence attracts confidence.

Step 5   **Leave Your House**
          You might not know where the man of your dreams is yet, but you know where he's not: your living room! Get out to where you can attract him.

Step 6   **Flirt, Flirt, Flirt!**
          Use the power of the Shy Eye Flirt. Be interested and interesting. Have fun.

Step 7   **You've Got a Date! Now What?**
          Dazzle him, discover him, and check your dealbreakers. And of course, keep flirting!

Step 8   **Be True To Yourself**
          Don't settle, because you deserve the best. Don't worry, because worry attracts worry. Live, grow, evolve, and enjoy. Work the 8 steps, and let no one rain on your parade.

Romance is around the corner for you!

978-0-595-67456-5
0-595-67456-9